I0901490

RAISED TO STAY

Devotional

NATALIE RUNION

RAISED TO STAY

Devotional

A 40-DAY JOURNEY FROM HURT TO HOLY

150 YEARS STRONG
DAVID C COOK

RAISED TO STAY DEVOTIONAL
Published by David C Cook
4050 Lee Vance Drive
Colorado Springs, CO 80918 U.S.A.

Integrity Music Limited, a Division of David C Cook
Brighton, East Sussex BN1 2RE, England

DAVID C COOK®, the graphic circle C logo and related marks
are registered trademarks of David C Cook.

All rights reserved. Except for brief excerpts for review purposes,
no part of this book may be reproduced or used in any form
without written permission from the publisher.

Unless otherwise noted, all Scripture quotations are taken from the Holy Bible, New Living Translation, copyright © 1996, 2015 by Tyndale House Foundation. Used by permission of Tyndale House Publishers, Carol Stream, Illinois 60188. All rights reserved. Scripture quotations marked ESV are taken from the ESV® Bible (The Holy Bible, English Standard Version®), copyright © 2001 by Crossway, a publishing ministry of Good News Publishers. Used by permission. All rights reserved; MSG are taken from THE MESSAGE, copyright © 1993, 2018 by Eugene H. Peterson. Used by permission of NavPress, represented by Tyndale House Publishers. All rights reserved; NIV are taken from the Holy Bible, New International Version®, NIV®. Copyright © 1973, 2011 by Biblica, Inc.™ Used by permission of Zondervan. All rights reserved worldwide. www.zondervan.com. The "NIV" and "New International Version" are trademarks registered in the United States Patent and Trademark Office by Biblica, Inc.™; NKJV are taken from the New King James Version®. Copyright © 1982 by Thomas Nelson. Used by permission. All rights reserved; NLV are taken from the *New Life Version*, copyright © 1969 and 2003. Used by permission of Barbour Publishing, Inc., Uhrichsville, Ohio 44683. All rights reserved; and NRSVA are taken from the New Revised Standard Version Bible: Anglicised Edition, copyright © 1989, 1995 the Division of Christian Education of the National Council of the Churches of Christ in the United States of America. Used by permission. All rights reserved.

Library of Congress Control Number 2025945179
ISBN 978-0-8307-9075-3
eISBN 978-0-8307-9076-0

© 2026 Natalie Ryan Runion
Published in association with the literary agency of WordServe
Literary Group, Ltd., www.wordserveliterary.com.

The Team: Susan McPherson, Stephanie Bennett, Jack Campbell, Susan Murdock
Cover Design: Joe Cavazos and James Hershberger
Cover Author Bio Photo: Ashlee Kay Photography
Interior Photos: Getty Images

Printed in the United States of America
First Edition 2026

1 2 3 4 5 6 7 8 9 10

091725

At David C Cook, we equip the local church around the corner and around the globe to make disciples. Come see how we are working together. Discover more. Be the difference. Visit DavidCCook.org/Donate.

Contents

Introduction

I SAID yes to Jesus when I was seven years old at the foot of my little white four-poster bed. I can still feel the cold hardwood floors on my knobby knees and smell the fresh laundry detergent from my lace comforter, an inch from my nose as I prayed with my mom by my side. Since that Sunday night in 1986, I have continued to give Jesus my yes. At times I've given it to him with a reluctant sigh and other times like a wrapped birthday gift shyly hidden behind my back. There have been days I've whispered my yes, other days I've roared it into the heavens, but one thing is for sure: picking up our cross and casting our nets and everything else that comes with being a disciple of Jesus Christ is not for the faint of heart.

When I look around me, when I take inventory of my life, there are many who started out beside me on this journey with Jesus who are no longer running their race. The cross became too heavy, the cost too high, the pain unbearable, the betrayal too deep, and while some simply left a church or ministry, others walked away from their faith altogether.

They couldn't stay.

It was this heartbreaking reality coupled with my own season of questioning why I shouldn't quit that the Lord began to challenge me to write to the wondering, wandering, wrestling about my own relationship with the church and God's people. Using black boxes to frame my white text, I showed up on social media even on the days I most wanted to quit. In this forum I shared what God was teaching me through his Word, my experiences as a pastor's kid turned pastor, and other believers.

The black boxes gave language to Christians around the globe consisting of different denominations, languages, ages, lifetime Christ followers, and brand-new believers, opening conversations that had once felt taboo and shedding light on issues many were too embarrassed to address. As these conversations grew, those on the cusp of quitting found freedom and healing—a movement began.

What started out as a small Instagram account of relatives and close friends became a community of hundreds of thousands of "Stayers" honest in their struggles and desperate for a reason to hold on—to Jesus, to each other.

The black boxes have been shared millions of times, quietly between coworkers and friends and publicly on church platforms streaming around the world. And just like our journey with Jesus, they tell of adventure through the hurt, the hard, the hope, and the holy, which we can only truly encounter by staying through it all and allowing God to turn all things out for our good and his glory.

In the years that followed, I wanted to quit more times than I care to confess. As I spent time in the Scriptures and prayer, as well as in worship and intercession, I shared with the Raised to Stay community what I was learning, and many times my black boxes were scrutinized, used as weapons rather than a sweet balm of healing, and my inbox overflowed with the angry, confused, and bitter.

It would have been easy to grow angry with the church and its people in the daily ambushes of nasty comments and stories of abuse at the hands of shepherds who should be protecting the sheep.

Rather, my anger turned to anguish, and my heart began to break for the wounded and the weary. I stayed, I continued writing the black boxes and showing up in the tenderness of the brokenhearted, believing that if I stayed, maybe I could encourage one more to hold on just a day longer.

The truth is, anyone can quit.

But sticking it out, not giving up, holding on, finishing what we start, that's hard work. Jesus modeled it for us on the cross, for the joy set before him, remaining in position. His crucifixion was the start of a resurrection.

What you think is about to kill you is often an invitation to new life.

He didn't quit on us.

We won't quit on him.

This book is for the Stayers, those who have journeyed through the black and white of the hurt and the hard and stayed to see the brilliance of color in the hope and the holy. This walk with Jesus isn't for the faint of heart.

Oh! How brave it is to stay!

Natalie

FOR thirty-three years Jesus called earth his home. He wasn't born a king in a palace with a crib and a royal guard to watch over him. He was delivered humbly and lowly from the womb of his mother, Mary, into the filthy sanctuary of a manger surrounded by the sounds of cattle and the exhausted breaths of the woman who had carried and just delivered the Son of God.

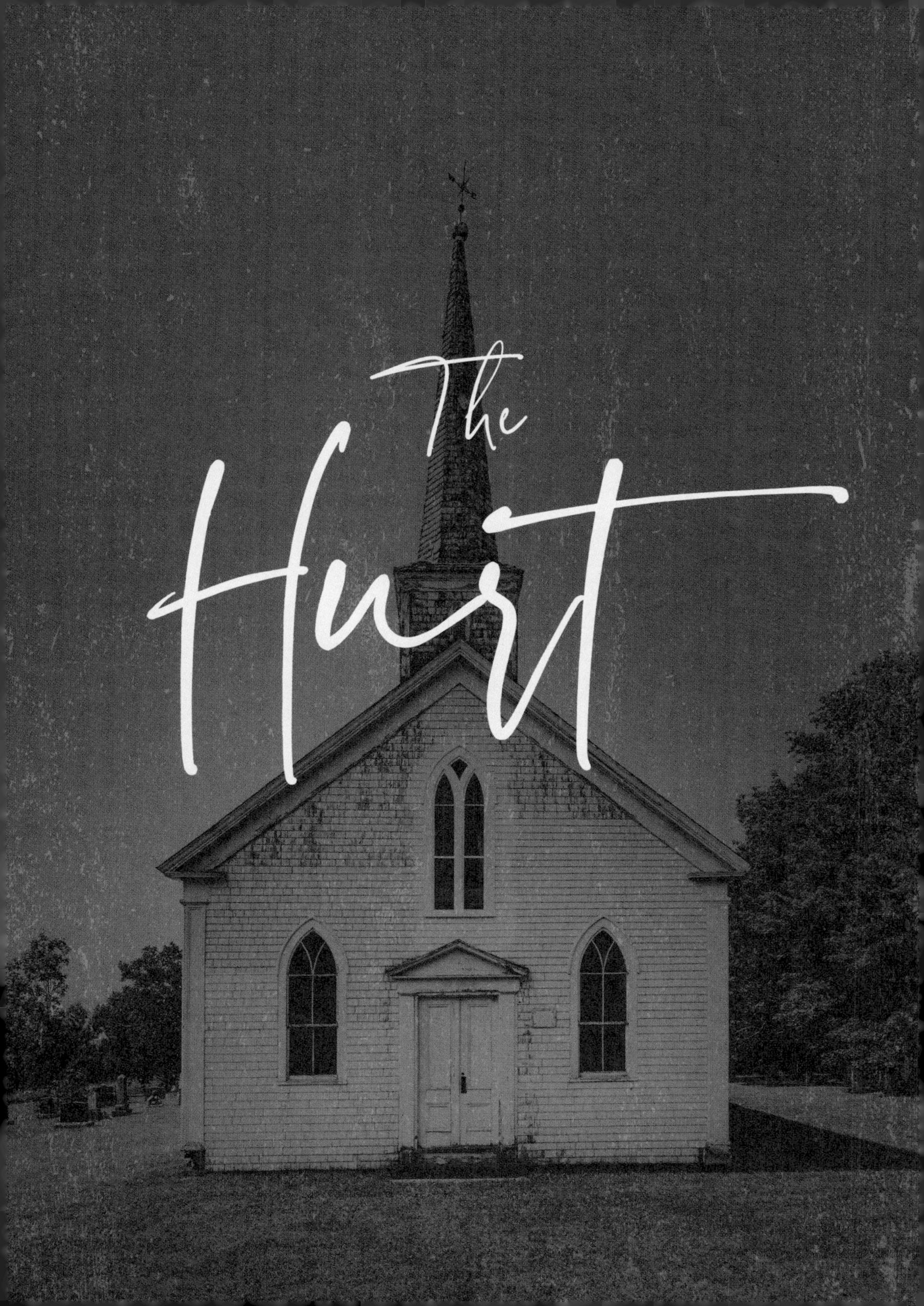
The Hurt

"Be it unto me as you have said" was her humble response to the angel who came to visit with the news that she, a virgin, would carry and give birth to the Savior of the world. Nine months of stares ... her own fiancé, Joseph, planning to quietly divorce her to avoid public shame until an angel appeared to him in a dream to reveal the divine plan. Nine months of being misunderstood ... her belly growing as those around her speculated of this immaculate conception, all of heaven simultaneously groaning in anticipation of the long-awaited Messiah.

Even in the womb, Jesus was introduced to the hurt that is humanity.

Protected and nurtured by his earthly mother and father, his personal ministry wouldn't even begin until he was thirty years old. In just three years, Jesus would find twelve men to be his disciples, traveling town to town speaking to those who would gather with the good new message of the Kingdom of God calling the people to repentance for the forgiveness of their sins. In just three years he would come up against some of his greatest critics, not the sinners, but those who believed they were saints, the Pharisees, who for the most part rejected Jesus and everything he taught to those who would listen. The religious would be among those to hurt our Jesus, leading him to trial and eventually his execution on the cross.

How beautiful is it that even in betrayal, Jesus was teaching his disciples and the crowds to love their enemies. Even now he sings these same words over you and me, reminding us to bless those who curse us, to pray for those who betray us, to forgive those who have trespassed against us, and to release them back into the hands of their Creator.

In Matthew 5:44, Jesus says, "But I say, love your enemies! Pray for those who persecute you!" In other passages he tells us to "love your enemies" and "do good to those who hate you" (Luke 6:27), and Romans 12:19 teaches that as his beloved, revenge will never bring revival in his words, "Do not take revenge, my dear friends, but leave room for God's wrath, for it is written: 'It is mine to avenge; I will repay,' says the Lord" (NIV).

From the floor of a dusty stable, where he was cradled in his mother's arms, to the darkened hill on Calvary, where he was held by the sins of the world, Jesus was no stranger to pain. With nails in his hands, his side pierced, a crown of thorns pressed into his brow, he looked out over a jeering crowd of sinners, cynics, skeptics, and saints. We hear what hurt sounds like from the heart of our Savior:

"Father, forgive them, for they don't know what they are doing" (Luke 23:34).

"My God, my God, why have you forsaken me?" (Matthew 27:46 NIV).

"Truly I tell you, today you will be with me in paradise" (Luke 23:43 NIV).

"Woman, behold your son!" and "Behold your mother!" (John 19:26–27 NKJV).

"I thirst!" (John 19:28 NKJV).

"It is finished!" (John 19:30).

"Father, into your hands I commend my spirit" (Luke 23:46 NRSVA).

As Jesus took his final breath, lifting himself up onto those nails to fill his punctured lungs with one last gulp of earthly air, the whole earth grew dark, and for a moment Satan thought he had won.

In what might be the greatest plot twist of all time, this crucifixion was the start of a resurrection.

Raised to Stay

Day 01

IN 2019, I went for a walk with the Lord and forty years of frustrations with the church and God's people came pouring out of me through prayerful tears. I had been a pastor's kid and then gone into full-time ministry. Forty years felt like a good holy number to ask God if I could tap out and quit. My heart was broken over my own hurts and betrayals but also grieved for those we had lost, fellow brothers and sisters who were so deeply wounded by God's people that they had chosen to walk away not only from the church, but from God himself.

During this walk, I heard the phrase "Raised to Stay" as if written in bold black letters across my heart. Not fully understanding what it meant, I ran home and wrote my first black box with white text on Instagram, and a movement of Stayers was born. This word, *stay*, doesn't mean we stay in harmful or abusive environments, but that we abide with Jesus and stay connected to his vine even when the winds of life try to blow us off. I know the church hurt you. I know people betrayed you. I am sorry the church hasn't always been safe for you. But you can rest in the truth that God is with you and for you, and even in hurt and betrayal, we can stay connected to Jesus and allow him to continue to produce good fruit through us even in the strongest of storms.

I'm sorry you were hurt by people in the church. Don't give up. You were raised to stay.

> "I am the vine; you are the branches. If you remain in me and I in you, you will bear much fruit; apart from me you can do nothing. If you do not remain in me, you are like a branch that is thrown away and withers; such branches are picked up, thrown into the fire and burned. If you remain in me and my words remain in you, ask whatever you wish, and it will be done for you. This is to my Father's glory, that you bear much fruit, showing yourselves to be my disciples." John 15:5–8 (NIV)

Abide: What does staying or abiding with Jesus mean to you?

I’m sorry you were hurt by people in the church. Don’t give up. You were raised to stay.

Sticks and Stones

Day 02

I KNOW what they said about you hurt …

I know the look of tainted treasure and lost equity. I know the sound of questioning identity based off another's opinion.

I know what poison feels like on fresh roots learning to grow again and the difficulty of nursing wilted petals that finally broke through rocky ground wanting desperately to believe new soil would produce new hope.

But God comes to you now with redemption, because what was said is never as powerful as who he says you are and whose you are, a child of God. His truth throws light on their shade. Don't grow weary of busting through dead places to bring life. Don't stop shining because you heard you shine too brightly. Let people talk and let God defend. Know your God. Know your soil. Unapologetically grow. Don't stop growing because someone didn't like your bloom.

"Blessed is the one who does not walk in step with the wicked or stand in the way that sinners take or sit in the company of mockers, but whose delight is in the law of the LORD, and who meditates on his law day and night. That person is like a tree planted by streams of water, which yields its fruit in season and whose leaf does not wither—whatever they do prospers." Psalm 1:1–3 (NIV)

Rewrite: What has been spoken over you that isn't from the Father? Who does God say you are in his Word?

Unapologetically grow. Don't stop growing because someone didn't like your bloom.

Can't Buy Me Love

Day 03

ONE of the greatest risks we will take in life is on each other; love is costly.

We can only be hurt by people we love. Loved. Will love. Every single time I've wanted to quit ministry or leave the church it was because my heart got broken. People will make you crazy. People will drive you mad. People will break you, try you, pull you in a million directions you never wanted to go, yet you'll go because love is powerful. And when we lose love, when trust is lost, when covenants are broken, we feel left alone to pick up the shattered remains.

But God loves a good remnant. He knows what to do with us when we've been torn apart by betrayal, tragedy, disaster. He takes what's left and rebuilds, restores, renews, reactivates, if we can acknowledge loss without fully deconstructing. Ministry is loving people, and people are a risky business. Jesus took the greatest risk of all in laying down his life for his friends. For you and for me. And he asks us to do the same. No greater love …

So, here's to broken hearts and disappointment. May our leftover pieces form a tapestry that tells a story of loving well, forgiving often, and taking risks on one another. You will be my greatest earthly risk. And God, my eternal reward.

> "This is my commandment: Love each other in the same way I have loved you. There is no greater love than to lay down one's life for one's friends. You are my friends if you do what I command." John 15:12–14

Count the cost: How has God shown his great love for you in your life?

You will be my greatest earthly risk. And God, my eternal reward.

Don't Let Your Judas Keep You from Your Jesus

Day 04

YOU won't like this one. I rarely talk to the runners, but I'm a fellow runner, like the runaway bride but more like the runaway church member. It's easier to run than to stay, this I know well. And I don't mean just in a physical church building because God knows sometimes the best thing to do is remove ourselves from toxic situations or take a sabbatical or rest.

I'm talking about those running from God. Those who have been looking for excuses to flee an Egypt that wasn't meant to hold us captive but challenge us to grow up, speak out, learn, and travail. To push. To groan. He has something for each of us to birth for his glory. But some of us, we straight up fled the scene because someone hurt us, wronged us.

We have all been hurt; we have all hurt others. We've all been wronged, talked about, betrayed, overlooked, misjudged—including Jesus. I'm so glad Jesus didn't run away. He took on the cross, for the joy set before him. Because anyone can run, hide, wallow in self-pity, but it takes true grit to stay and watch God make it right. For the joy set before him. For the joy set before us. Because when God makes something right, there is restoration and healing and forgiveness and change and newness and beauty and hope again.

Those we've wronged, those who have wronged us, either find forgiveness or God frees us from the chains of bitterness and unforgiveness ... both are worth contending for in the body of Christ. He makes all things new. He will make all things right. But if we run, we won't see the redemption.

If we let Judas keep us from our Jesus, we will never know abundant life. If someone has wronged you, if a church has hurt you, if a leader has wounded you, don't run from the One who can make it right. The enemy wants us on the run. Our Father calls us to abide. And he is faithful.

> "Therefore, since we are surrounded by such a huge crowd of witnesses to the life of faith, let us strip off every weight that slows us down, especially the sin that so easily trips us up. And let us run with endurance the race God has set before us. We do this by keeping our eyes on Jesus, the champion who initiates and perfects our faith. Because of the joy awaiting him, he endured the cross, disregarding its shame. Now he is seated in the place of honor beside God's throne. Think of all the hostility he endured from sinful people; then you won't become weary and give up. After all, you have not yet given your lives in your struggle against sin." Hebrews 12:1–4

Forgive: Who have you let keep you from trusting Jesus or his Church?

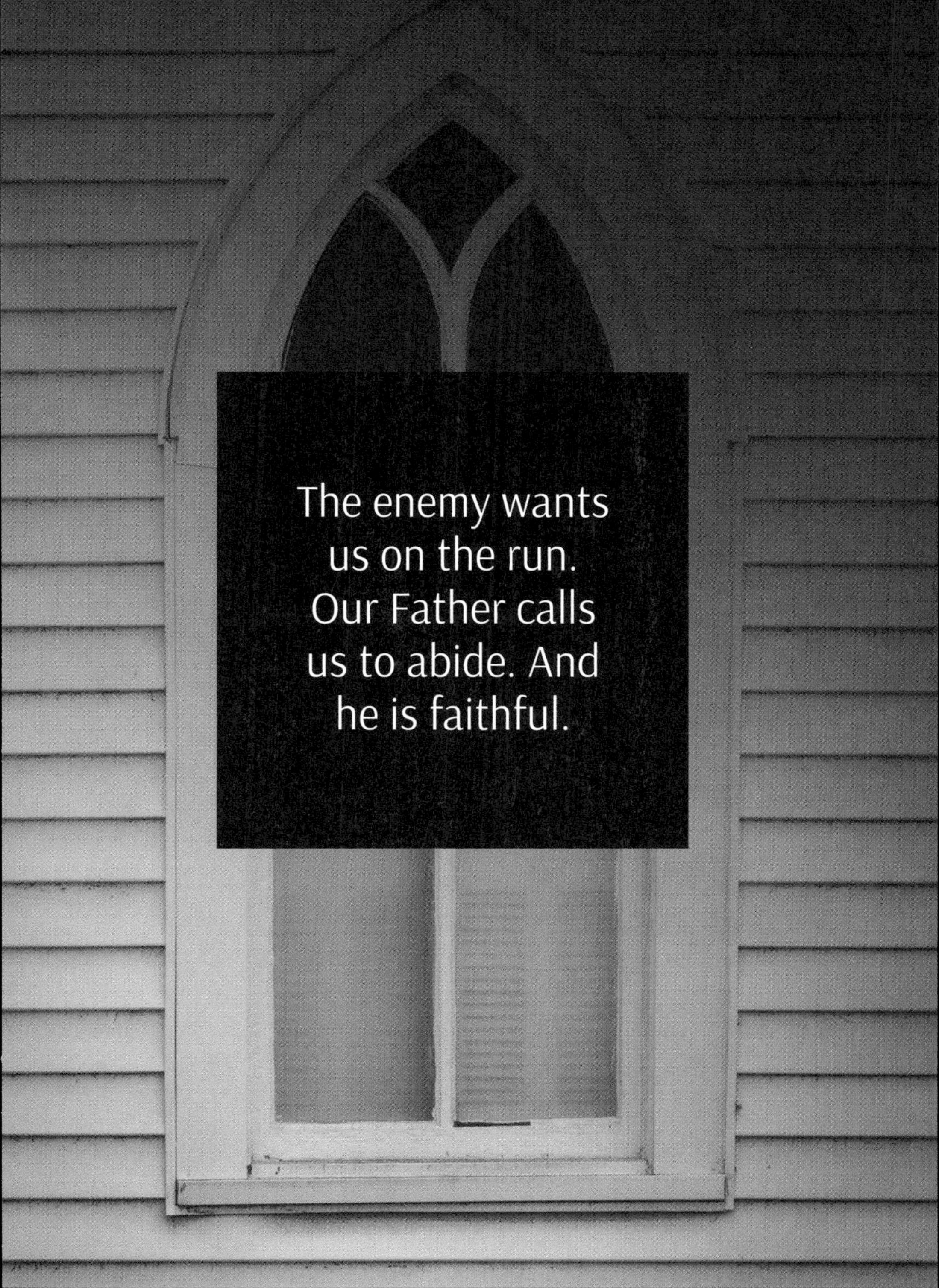

The enemy wants us on the run. Our Father calls us to abide. And he is faithful.

Come On In

Day 05

FOR those forced into new beginnings after a traumatic ending …

God sees you tiptoeing back into the water, testing the temperature and wondering if those around you will make you sink or help you swim. He knows you're scared to try again, to trust again, after nearly drowning as others watched. It hurts when nobody tries to save you; self-preservation is a terrible life preserver. He is patient as you reemerge from uncharted waters; he assigns angels like lifeguards as you remember how to keep your head above the waves.

How brave it is to let others see you in distress and trust they will come to your rescue before they save themselves. I know it's easier to stay onshore, but there is beauty in catching our breath and jumping back in. It's always bitter cold at first, but I promise it will warm up. Hear the family of God call to you from the depths, "Come on in, the water is just right!" Bitter endings can lead to holy beginnings. COME. ON. IN.

"The thought of my suffering and homelessness is bitter beyond words. I will never forget this awful time, as I grieve over my loss. Yet I still dare to hope when I remember this: The faithful love of the LORD never ends! His mercies never cease. Great is his faithfulness; his mercies begin afresh each morning. I say to myself, 'The LORD is my inheritance; therefore, I will hope in him!'" Lamentations 3:19–24

Enter in: What would it look like for you to tiptoe back into the waters of ministry, the church, or your relationship with Jesus?

Bitter endings
can lead to holy
beginnings.
COME. ON. IN.

Revenge Won't Expedite the Promises of God

Day 06

I HAVE never fully understood why David didn't kill Saul when he had the chance. He had a perfect shot at him, and yet he only took the edge of his cloak. Because I'll be honest, I've been betrayed by leaders in my life, and I've done some straight-up murder in my heart. Have you ever thought, *If that person weren't in my way or making my life miserable, I'd finally get to do and be everything God has for me!?* I'm guessing that for a split second, David, in his humanity and hurt, wanted Saul dead. Yet in David's humility, as a man after God's heart, he understood killing someone wouldn't get him any closer to God's promise that he would be king. Revenge does not expedite the promises of God. God had a whole plan for David that couldn't be stopped by a dysfunctional leader on a power trip.

The same goes for you and me. Whatever God has for you is for you. We will all have bad leaders, and at times be bad leaders and the good news is no one is powerful enough to stop the promises of God. David even says upon choosing to spare Saul's life, "For who can remain innocent after attacking the LORD's anointed one?" Do not allow murder to enter your heart in pursuit of the promises of God. He fights for us every single time, and the only way we can move from the cave to the promised position of God is to stay faithful even when we have been betrayed.

Leave your Saul to God. Obedience is your mission.

> "'Now's your opportunity!' David's men whispered to him. 'Today the LORD is telling you, "I will certainly put your enemy into your power, to do with as you wish."' So David crept forward and cut off a piece of the hem of Saul's robe. But then David's conscience began bothering him because he had cut Saul's robe. He said to his men, 'The LORD forbid that I should do this to my lord the king. I shouldn't attack the LORD's anointed one, for the LORD himself has chosen him.' So David restrained his men and did not let them kill Saul." 1 Samuel 24:4–7

Onward: Write a letter to your Saul or your Judas, then spend time in prayer asking the Lord to heal the hurt so you can move forward in freedom.

Leave your Saul to God. Obedience is your mission.

Sunday Struggles

Day 07

IF you're having a hard time trusting again, trying again, know that God isn't caught off guard by your hesitation. He isn't offended by your defense or inconvenienced by your questions. He was there when you fell, by your side when you got pushed down, near when you felt uninvited and unseen. He isn't disappointed in your discouragement. Rather, he is teaching that your trust should not be in man but in your God, who does not lie, delay, or come up short on his promises. Our hope is in him, the one who picks us up and fixes our feet on a firm foundation.

We will fall again. We will be let down, left, and feel lost doing good work, but we're never alone. Trusting again, trying again, invites the Holy Spirit into sacred spaces where we surrender our weakness for his power. I know you're tired of picking up the broken pieces of your heart, but God's anointing is more powerful than your brokenness. His light shines with great beauty through our fragments; he loves remnants.

It's okay if you're not ready to get up just yet, but don't stay down for too long. Falling isn't failure, resting isn't quitting, waiting isn't weakness. But you have an assignment with your name on it, and God knows how to restore us as we run. You will trust again; you will try again. Take a moment to clean yourself up, and then put the enemy on notice. You aren't quitting. You're just catching your breath.

> "Let us think of ways to motivate one another to acts of love and good works. And let us not neglect our meeting together, as some people do, but encourage one another, especially now that the day of his return is drawing near." Hebrews 10:24–25

Re-entry: What is keeping you from fully engaging with your church community?

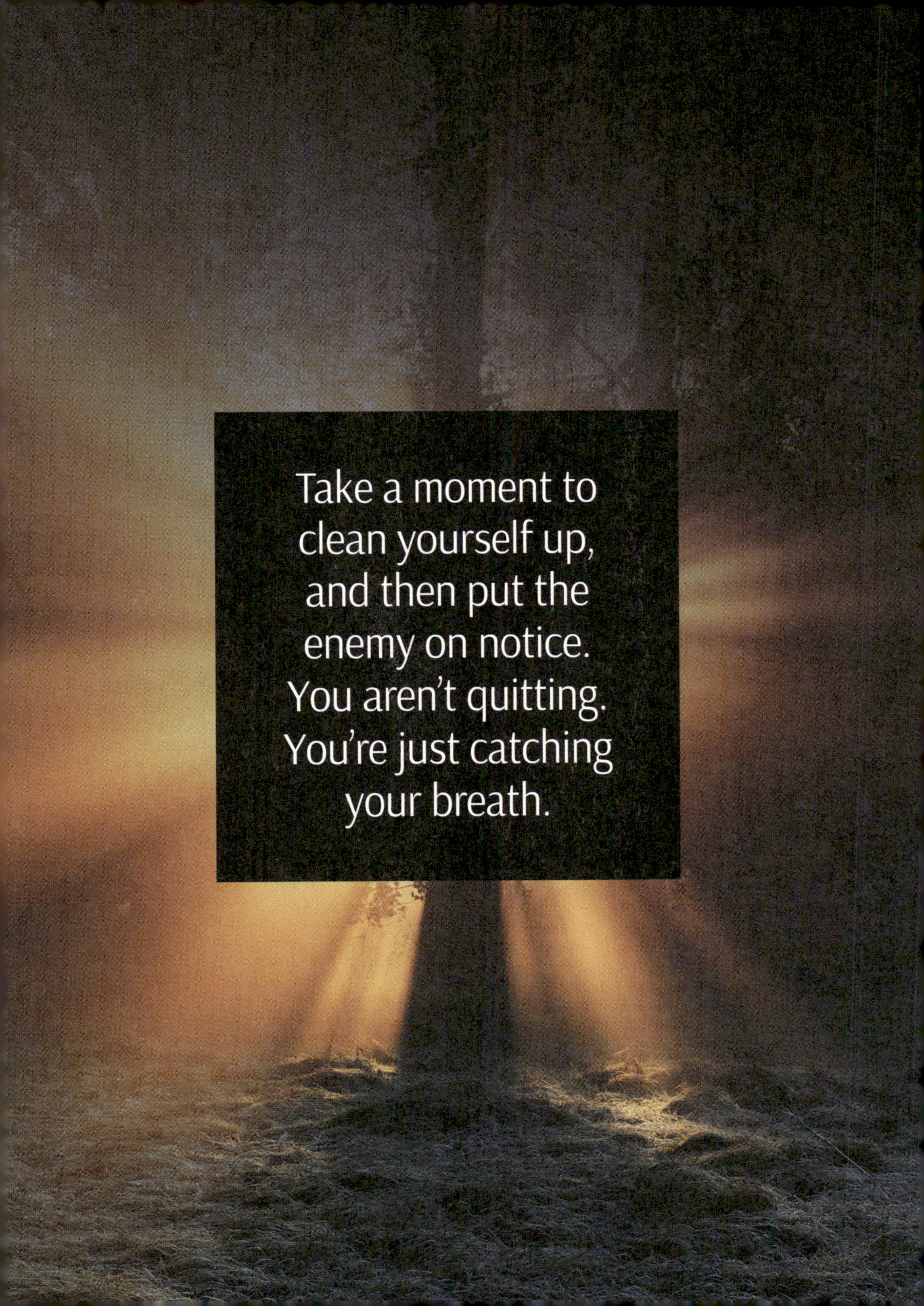

Take a moment to clean yourself up, and then put the enemy on notice. You aren't quitting. You're just catching your breath.

Porchlights and Prodigals

Day 08

PRODIGALS aren't projects, they are incoming miracles.

For those waiting for a prodigal to return, you are in good company. As the Church, we sit at the windows of our sanctuaries and homes praying for the returns of sons and daughters who have wandered off, the porchlights of our hearts burning bright day and night. However, there isn't a church program or holiday event powerful enough to woo them away from the world who was a ready receiver of those the church rejected. Only God, the holy hound of heaven, is tracking their every move and dispatching angels to stand watch over them as we whisper their names in intercession and worship into the night. He sees them. He knows their names. He is with them.

And as they walk through our doors, they are not projects to be won over, rather long-awaited miracles, and we celebrate with all of eternity when one comes home. Do not grow weary in the waiting. Fix yourself at the doorpost of your home, and we as the Church will do the same. We believe every miracle is on their way home. We won't stop praying and believing until every seat at the table is filled once again. Together, we are praying the prodigals home.

> "When he was still a long way off, his father saw him. His heart pounding, he ran out, embraced him, and kissed him. The son started his speech: 'Father, I've sinned against God, I've sinned before you; I don't deserve to be called your son ever again.' But the father wasn't listening. He was calling to the servants, 'Quick. Bring a clean set of clothes and dress him. Put the family ring on his finger and sandals on his feet. Then get a prize-winning heifer and roast it. We're going to feast! We're going to have a wonderful time! My son is here—given up for dead and now alive! Given up for lost and now found!' And they began to have a wonderful time." Luke 15:20–24 (MSG)

Pray them home: Do you have a prodigal in your life? Write down their name and journal a blessing over them or a scripture, then spend some time in prayer.

We won't stop praying and believing until every seat at the table is filled once again. Together, we are praying the prodigals home.

Out of Your Belly ...

Day 09

DO you want to know what nearly broke me? The Church who built me. Then the Lord asking me to surrender my identity and what I felt I was owed. It was learning that what I thought I was created to give birth to wasn't going to look like what I'd envisioned for twenty years. I have mourned what I thought was a spiritual miscarriage, and in just the last year, I felt that stirring of new life flowing from the depths of my belly.

Sometimes we don't quit because we're mad or frustrated or offended ... we leave a church or position because we're heartbroken. Yet it's here in this place that we learn God's anointing is greater than our brokenness and what he wants to deliver through us is bigger than a talent, gift, or hobby. It's a Kingdom assignment delivered only after great sacrifice and labor. We must stay through loss and disappointment and unmet expectations to know the true joy of redemption, new breath, and to hear the fresh cries of what we've always been called to carry.

There will come a day when you will feel your womb leap again with new life. It will be when you least expect it, on an ordinary day while you're taking steps of obedience and walking by faith, not by what you can see. Keep showing up with expectant anticipation and waiting on the Lord. Brokenhearted, take courage. What you carry might not be what you expected, but it's from the Holy Spirit and it is beautiful.

What broke your heart is about to make your womb leap.

> "My child, never forget the things I have taught you. Store my commands in your heart. If you do this, you will live many years, and your life will be satisfying. Never let loyalty and kindness leave you! Tie them around your neck as a reminder. Write them deep within your heart. Then you will find favor with both God and people, and you will earn a good reputation. Trust in the LORD with all your heart; do not depend on your own understanding. Seek his will in all you do, and he will show you which path to take." Proverbs 3:1–6

New life: Has a dream or hope felt deferred or even dead? Speak life over it now! Dream again, out of your belly will flow new life as you surrender it back to the Lord.

What you carry
might not be what
you expected,
but it's from the
Holy Spirit and
it is beautiful.

Blessed Are Those Who Mourn ...

Day 10

IT'S okay to mourn what was lost, to lament what could have been yet will never be ...

It's good to sit in our night and demand a morning; it keeps us looking to the sky. You are allowed to weep and shake your fists in frustration, to pen letters you'll never send, asking for forgiveness—and dare I say, revenge—that will never come. There isn't a healing prescription for this kind of pain, only the remains of those who have been here before us, and if we let them, they will pull us down into their shallow graves to die beside them. So don't stand still for too long. Run ... even if there are tears streaming down your face as you pick up the broken pieces of your shattered heart that you didn't think could break again. There are miracles in every remnant. Don't leave a single shard behind; God is making something beautiful from it all.

Take every disappointment, every unmet expectation, each broken promise and betrayal, and turn them into kindling for a new day.

Use them to feed your fire inside to preach the Gospel you have been called to carry.

May God exchange that robe of grief for a garment of praise, that sackcloth for clothing of joy. It's coming, a new dawn fresh with mercy, so be honest with the darkness as you wait for the light. He keeps track of all our sorrows. He has recorded each one in his book. He has collected all our tears in his bottle. Every arrow that has been aimed in your direction has fallen short.

> "I'm proud to praise God, proud to praise GOD. Fearless now, I trust in God; what can mere mortals do to me? God, you did everything you promised, and I'm thanking you with all my heart. You pulled me from the brink of death, my feet from the cliff-edge of doom. Now I stroll at leisure with God in the sunlit fields of life." Psalm 56:10–13 (MSG)

Let go: Name those who have hurt you and situations that have left you wounded. Now turn the mourning into praise and write out how God has shown up faithful even in disappointment.

He keeps track of all our sorrows. He has recorded each one in his book. He has collected all our tears in his bottle.

IN his final breath, Jesus offered up the words "It is finished." He took the cup of God's wrath meant for you and me, swallowing its bitterness and shame. His head fell, his spirit surrendered, his work and mission on earth complete. Darkness enveloped the whole land; an earthquake shook the ground, splitting rocks and breaking open tombs and the curtain of the sanctuary was torn in two from top to bottom.

The Hard
FOR SALE

Behold, our Jesus, the final, precious sacrificial lamb.

Those three days between Jesus' crucifixion and resurrection must have felt like an eternity for the disciples and those who loved him. The anguish, sorrow, doubt, fear—every emotion—must have felt magnified without the comfort and wisdom of their teacher, pastor, son, and friend. I often think of Mary sitting outside his tomb, knowing her son lay wrapped in linens behind the boulder as a guard kept watch.

As Mary was mourning, I imagine the disciples wandering on the dirt roads they once walked with Jesus, playing the events of the last several weeks over and over in their heads. How had they missed the one who would betray them sitting among them all this time? Why didn't they stay and tarry with Jesus just a bit longer in the garden? Was Peter feeling guilt for denying knowing Jesus not once, not twice, but three times? Did he wish he had done more to that guard in the garden than just cut off his ear?

Were they reminiscing about the three years with their Savior? "This is where the blind man was healed! Remember?" "This is where we fed the five thousand. What a day!" "Remember when he walked on the water? Peter, tell us that story again."

When we reflect on the hard days between the crucifixion and resurrection, we are invited into our own time with Jesus, during the pain of betrayal, abuse, abandonment, of a public death without a third day in sight. It invites us to look back on our imperfect life, but when we trace the miracles and count the blessings, we realize that even in the hurt and the hard, we cannot deny what we have seen.

It invites us into sorrow for our sin and gratitude for God's grace.

We have walked and talked with Jesus, and we have been forever changed.

> On the third day the women took the spices they had prepared to the tomb, but they arrived to find the stone rolled away and Jesus nowhere to be seen. An angel appeared to them and asked a question I now ask you: "Why do you look for the living among the dead? He is not here; he has risen!" (Luke 24:5–6 NIV).

The angels reminded them of what Jesus said while he was still in Galilee: the Son of Man must be delivered over to the hands of sinners, be crucified, and on the third day be raised again, and in Luke 24:8 it tells us, "Then they remembered his words" (NIV).

God always finishes what he starts.

His promises are yes and amen.

Beloved, why are you looking for life in dead places? Why are you revisiting the place of your greatest pain and occupying the tombs where you once lay when you now have a chance at a hope and healing that can only come from Christ?

God has been with you in the hurt.

And today he is reminding you as he walks beside you, coaxing you out of your tomb, that even in the hard, he is faithful to complete the work—crucifixion to resurrection.

From Exile to an Exodus

Day 11

THE word *exodus* comes from the Greek word *exodos*, which means "the road out." Maybe you need to hear in this moment that what has felt like rejection was actually a holy rescue. What has felt like a season of exile was a stealthy mission of a good Father who loves you too much to let your need for acceptance lead to your captivity. God knows when it's time for a departure long before we sense a change. And we might have to wander in a wilderness for a while, but we will always find a parting sea and the promises of God fulfilled, because his promises are yes and amen. Nobody wants to go back to their Egypt, but we all have to revisit those areas that keep holding us prisoner so we can break free from the things keeping us from the Promised Land.

The mission before you requires a staff in one hand and the commandments of our God in the other, and not everyone will understand what you carry. So yes, you might feel isolated, but you are never alone. I know you want to belong. Rest in God's truth that you are beloved.

What felt like exile was actually an exodus. You weren't rejected, you were rescued.

> "Moses answered the people, 'Do not be afraid. Stand firm and you will see the deliverance the LORD will bring you today. The Egyptians you see today you will never see again. The LORD will fight for you; you need only to be still.'" Exodus 14:13–14 (NIV)

Rescued: How has God gone before you in this season?

What felt like exile was actually an exodus. You weren't rejected, you were rescued.

Desert Days

Day 12

THEY say by the time you are thirsty, you are already dehydrated. We feel hungry and fill up on snacks when our bodies aren't asking for carbohydrates and sugar, but rather water, pure H_2O. And how often we confuse hunger for thirst in seasons of abundance, rain, and blessings. We go to the pantry and grab what we want when we want it and temporarily satisfy cravings with weak substitutes.

But in the desert, in a drought where the cupboards are bare and the blessing seemingly withheld, we are left with our thirst. And the desert, this dry place, this barren space with few resources or anyone to bring us a snack, is where we start our search for water. Living water. No substitutes. No Diet Coke. No alcohol. No Netflix to take our mind off the pain. No social media to scroll through at night. It's there we long for streams that make glad the city of the Lord. For the still waters that will restore our soul. The desert loves us enough to tell us we're thirsty for a season with a promise that he's with us and it's for a purpose. Because it's in this place we're changed. Challenged. Convicted. Loved. Healed. Protected.

Provided for. Championed. Seen. It's in the desert we truly learn how to hunger and thirst for righteousness. Put down the Cheez-Its. Our God is sending manna.

I won't forsake the desert. It taught me how to look for living water.

> "O God, you are my God; I earnestly search for you. My soul thirsts for you; my whole body longs for you in this parched and weary land where there is no water. I have seen you in your sanctuary and gazed upon your power and glory. Your unfailing love is better than life itself; how I praise you! I will praise you as long as I live, lifting up my hands to you in prayer. You satisfy me more than the richest feast. I will praise you with songs of joy." Psalm 63:1–5

Refuel: What have you been filling up on to numb the pain of a hard season?

I won't forsake the desert. It taught me how to look for living water.

I'm Not Leaving, I'm Going

Day 13

I WAS in the tenth grade when my parents, who were pastoring their own church, allowed me to attend another church in our community. This was where I was starting to step into my calling. I think it was hard for some people in our congregation to understand that I wasn't leaving, I was going. But sometimes going looks like leaving when it's misunderstood. Going can look like quitting, abandoning, failing, or rejecting when the direction God is asking us to go doesn't come with a warranty, a five-year plan, or GPS.

Nobody can track us or describe our whereabouts. We look lost, unsure, or travel-weary, but it's here in the middle of nowhere that it gets good. It's in the going that we start building and getting creative. We can't hang on to our parents, we can't rely on a decade of experience or a fancy résumé or portfolio. When God takes us off course to blaze a new trail, it may look crazy and leave people scratching their heads, wondering why we'd leave the familiar for the unknown. But our discomfort and growing pains force a biblical maturity that comes with a spiritual adolescence.

I guess the only answer is I'd rather be in the unknown with Jesus than in the familiar without him. Like I told my dad at sixteen years old: I can safely sit in a pew and check boxes to make people happy, or I can go and do what I know God is asking me to do even if nobody understands it. And I'm eternally grateful he let me go.

Deep down, I think he knew that by letting me go I'd never want to leave. I wonder if some of us are afraid to go into the unknown because we've worked so hard and so long to be here. We're afraid to lose status—our reputation—but it's all meaningless if it's not where God wants us. Going isn't quitting or abandoning anything. It's releasing something that was good to grab hold of God's best. Though it's terrifying to let go, it's exhilarating to see what he has waiting on the other side of obedience.

Take it from someone who has spent the last several years going … you won't want to look back.

> "But don't just listen to God's word. You must do what it says. Otherwise, you are only fooling yourselves. For if you listen to the word and don't obey, it is like glancing at your face in a mirror. You see yourself, walk away, and forget what you look like. But if you look carefully into the perfect law that sets you free, and if you do what it says and don't forget what you heard, then God will bless you for doing it." James 1:22–25

Go: What is God inviting you into that might require going into something new?

Though it's
terrifying to let go,
it's exhilarating
to see what he
has waiting on
the other side
of obedience.

Don't Go Back

Day 14

THIS is for those considering going back to a place of familiarity even though God clearly called you out. Those thinking of returning to famine because it's familiar. Those who would rather crawl back to your abusers than sit in anonymity. Those who are tempted to return to dysfunction because you don't like the discomfort of the unknown. Those who have convinced yourselves you weren't enslaved but rather indentured servants. Those who believe it will be different this time.

God told you to go; don't make an eleven-day trip into forty years of wandering in the wilderness. He rescued you from that relationship, that church, that position, that situation; it wasn't an exile, it was an exodus. He got you out for a reason. Don't die disobedient. Don't live doubting God's promise. He said go. So don't look back.

Don't go back to Egypt just because you haven't reached the Promise Land.

"Pharaoh sent for Moses and Aaron during the night. 'Get out!' he ordered. 'Leave my people—and take the rest of the Israelites with you! Go and worship the LORD as you have requested. Take your flocks and herds, as you said, and be gone. Go, but bless me as you leave.' All the Egyptians urged the people of Israel to get out of the land as quickly as possible, for they thought, 'We will all die!' The Israelites took their bread dough before yeast was added. They wrapped their kneading boards in their cloaks and carried them on their shoulders. And the people of Israel did as Moses had instructed; they asked the Egyptians for clothing and articles of silver and gold. The LORD caused the Egyptians to look favorably on the Israelites, and they gave the Israelites whatever they asked for. So they stripped the Egyptians of their wealth!" Exodus 12:31–36

Eyes up: What are you tempted to return to out of fear or familiarity?

Don’t live doubting
God’s promise.
He said go.
So don’t look back.

Shipwrecks Happen. Get Back in the Boat.

Day 15

PAUL survived three shipwrecks. *Three* shipwrecks during his ministry. I have to ask, "Paul, why do you keep getting back in the boat?"

I don't know about you, but if I get queasy on a ride at the fair, I write off all things that spin, drop, or fly. But not Paul. He kept getting back in the boat and going out on the water because he knew what was required of him to fulfill his assignment.

I am challenged by looking at my last few shipwrecks ... and how with each one the temptation to quit has grown stronger. I didn't know if I had another one in me, another season of rebuilding something lost, another season of feeling stranded or isolated. It's easy to get so consumed fretting over broken bows and torn sails that we forget the indestructible Word of God is still screaming over our lives. That the Great Commission is still ringing out across the earth to get back in the boat and go, even if we find ourselves wrecked on the same island standing among familiar rubble. We learn to grieve it, rebuild it, and return to the boat with the Gospel in hand and our God riding with us.

Perhaps this has been your shipwreck season … as you were heading in one direction with the wind at your back only to be slammed against the rocks. You're collecting yourself and taking inventory of what was lost, but now it's time to map out the next adventure. And maybe that's why Paul kept getting back in the boat. Because he knew the reward was greater than the risk. Every single time he got back in the boat, he boasted in his weakness and revealed the strength of God, who would be made known everywhere he went.

It's time to get back in the boat. We've mourned long enough. We can beg the Lord all day long to make it all go away and to make life easier, but his response as he puts us back in the boat will always be "My grace is all you need …" Grab a life jacket. It's time to set sail.

"Three different times I begged the Lord to take it away. Each time he said, 'My grace is all you need. My power works best in weakness.' So now I am glad to boast about my weaknesses, so that the power of Christ can work through me. That's why I take pleasure in my weaknesses, and in the insults, hardships, persecutions, and troubles that I suffer for Christ. For when I am weak, then I am strong." 2 Corinthians 12:8–10

Don't quit: What is keeping you from getting back in the boat?

Grab a life jacket. It's time to set sail.

Be the Church

Day 16

WE'VE been so busy playing church, we have forgotten how to be the Church.

When I came off church staff—giving up the daily tasks that come with preparing for Sundays and every holiday and special event in between—I realized how busy we are doing church. I also saw how easy it was to play church and accept roles even when it felt like we were compromising values or convictions. Sundays come fast, and ready or not, church can become a game we're playing simply to survive.

I had forgotten what it was like to *be* the Church—in my community, as a normal mom, at the gym, or shopping in the grocery store—who saw needs and met them without a title but as a Christian. I forgot that church wasn't just a Sunday event.

For many of us, church is a ritual, and I suppose that is a first step in creating rhythms that get us in the door once a week. But what if it's intended to be so much more? What if we're missing out on being the Church because we've grown weary of playing a rehearsed part: show up, smile, drink some coffee, sit in service, clock out, do it again in a week? For those of us, learning to be the Church again will be a saving grace. It will remind us of our original yes and call us back into a position of abiding and not striving. I pray that for all of us: personal revival and a reminder of our assignment, not obligation.

> "So guard yourselves and God's people. Feed and shepherd God's flock—his church, purchased with his own blood—over which the Holy Spirit has appointed you as leaders." Acts 20:28

Be the church: How have you been playing church? What would it look like in this season of life to be the church?

But what if it's
intended to be
so much more?

It's So Hard to Say Goodbye

Day 17

LET the disciples be an example that we can lose a leader and stay on mission.

It's hard and often confusing when a pastor or leader leaves a church or organization. Whether their departure is due to a moral failure or simply another assignment, when we love our leaders, it is difficult to imagine doing ministry without them.

I think of the disciples after Jesus—their friend, pastor, and Messiah—ascended into heaven and left them with one mission: the Great Commission. I wonder if they had conflicting emotions as they oscillated between feeling mad, sad, confused, discouraged, frustrated, and scared, as well as challenged, eager, and ready for the mission ahead. What would they do? Where would they go?

If we stay in a church for any length of time, a leader will go. Even when we're celebrating and wishing them well, we still feel loss—maybe also hurt. It's even worse when we lose a leader to scandal or moral failure. We can feel betrayed or alternatively defensive of them if we called them friend. And the most confusing departures are when we aren't quite sure what happened; we just know they aren't around anymore.

None of it feels good. I'd like to think the empty tomb and seeing Jesus alive brought the disciples great comfort, but I imagine they wanted a few more adventures together. A few more miracles, another sign or perhaps a wonder.

We see the disciples launch out into their own ministries, their mission clear …

Go.

Make disciples.

And it's our mission too. No matter who comes and goes, rises or falls, stays or leaves, it doesn't change our God-given assignment.

The disciples didn't lose Jesus, though his ascension changed his position in their lives. They took what they had learned and boarded ships, sang hymns in prisons, traveled afar, and took with them the Good News.

Jesus is our greatest advocate to the Father, the Holy Spirit is our guide, and the Word of God is our weapon against fiery arrows from our enemy. We haven't been left, we have been anointed to proclaim good news to the poor, freedom for the prisoners, recovery of sight for the blind, and to set the oppressed free. Leaders will come and go. Jesus Christ is the same yesterday, today, and forever.

> "[Jesus] replied, 'The Father alone has the authority to set those dates and times, and they are not for you to know. But you will receive power when the Holy Spirit comes upon you. And you will be my witnesses, telling people about me everywhere—in Jerusalem, throughout Judea, in Samaria, and to the ends of the earth.' After saying this, he was taken up into a cloud while they were watching, and they could no longer see him. As they strained to see him rising into heaven, two white-robed men suddenly stood among them. 'Men of Galilee,' they said, 'why are you standing here staring into heaven? Jesus has been taken from you into heaven, but someday he will return from heaven in the same way you saw him go!'" Acts 1:7–11

Let them go: How has losing a leader you loved impacted your life, ministry, or relationships?

Leaders will come
and go. Jesus
Christ is the same
yesterday, today,
and forever.

The Power of an Apology

Day 18

"I AM sorry I hurt you, please forgive me."

I have preached a lot of messages and led a lot of songs. I have seen sanctuaries and conference centers packed with people for revivals and church events, whether from pastors bringing their best or off-the-chart productions. But I've never witnessed the power of the Holy Spirit like sitting across from another brother or sister and speaking these words: "Please forgive me." I have spoken them in living rooms and coffee shops, over the phone and in groups, and the moment the reconciling words of our Father enter into the most dysfunctional church families, chains are broken. Even if the response isn't immediate trust or restoration, Satan loses his power to bring offense and division. I've never left one of these conversations without encountering the tangible presence of God.

We spend a lot of time crafting set lists and sermons, but I can assure you that humbling ourselves as leaders is our most favorable position and platform in the eyes of God. Even if we feel we've done nothing wrong, even if the exact words are hard to find, knowing we have hurt someone and asking for their forgiveness brings clarity to confusion and light into darkness. Even if we still lose people or a relationship, even if we don't get the desired outcome, there is more Jesus in repentance and reconciliation than the most powerful sermon. Because where there is unity, it commands the Lord's blessing.

I know hearing this from pastors has healed parts of me I didn't know were still wounded. We all need to know this sermon of "I am sorry," the freedom of "forgive me," the release of being forgiven and forgiving. These words are like a sweet balm that can restore a life we didn't know was on the fringe. Preach that message before all others.

> "Get rid of all bitterness, rage, anger, harsh words, and slander, as well as all types of evil behavior. Instead, be kind to each other, tenderhearted, forgiving one another, just as God through Christ has forgiven you." Ephesians 4:31–32

Release it: Who do you need to forgive who has never offered you an apology? Write a prayer of forgiveness for them even if it's hard. This is part of healing.

We all need to know this sermon of “I am sorry,” the freedom of “forgive me,” the release of being forgiven and forgiving.

The Ministry of Presence

Day 19

ONE of the hardest journeys we will take as Christians is moving from being served to serving others with purity of heart and intentions. We will know we are truly ministering to others when we spend more time walking with people through their Egypts than we spend in our personal Promised Lands.

Several years ago, I had lunch with a young leader who had just resigned from their position at their local church, and when I asked why they had decided to go, their response was honest.

"It wasn't fun anymore."

I wasn't surprised. After all, we have a new generation of leaders who watch social media thinking ministry is more like Disneyland than a mission field, and then they show up on a Sunday morning only to receive an orange vest to direct cars in a gravel parking lot and a list of congregants who need meals and hospital visits.

If I have learned anything in serving the local church, it is this: If you stay through the hard of transition and the tension of unknowns and the unexpected, the gift comes in baptizing a prodigal, witnessing a miracle baby born after years of infertility, or officiating a funeral of a saint you hugged every Sunday morning. The deserts come before the rain and so many of us quit before we get to see the face of a friend find freedom or a complete stranger say yes to Jesus.

Our personal Promised Lands look like what we want and who we want to become. When we arrive there, it's easy to camp out and get comfortable, but it's just a mirage. You won't be happy there; it's made up of false summits and man-made resources.

But when we walk with a person through their Egypt, we get to celebrate an exodus so sacred it never gets old—being part of someone's miracle. If we quit, we won't get to see that loving and serving people is the greatest adventure with Jesus.

We all get tired; we want the fun more than the famine. Just because it's hard doesn't mean it's wrong; some of the most beautiful Promised Lands I've experienced weren't my own.

> "Therefore, go and make disciples of all the nations, baptizing them in the name of the Father and the Son and the Holy Spirit. Teach these new disciples to obey all the commands I have given you. And be sure of this: I am with you always, even to the end of the age." Matthew 28:19–20

Presence: Who needs your ministry of presence right now? Pray for them by name and ask the Lord for creative ways you can be Jesus to them in this season of life.

Just because it's hard doesn't mean it's wrong; some of the most beautiful Promised Lands I've experienced weren't my own.

Uninvited

Day 20

OUR faith will command action: moving states, changing positions, unraveling from toxic religious beliefs and systems, leaving and cleaving … going and changing. There will be people who will cheer us on in our wrestling, wandering, and wondering, and those who will demand explanations when we ourselves are still searching for answers. Not everyone can go with us; sometimes God asks us to travel quietly for a bit, and other times he gives us our twelve who are committed to our mission.

The voices from our past will often demand a vote in our decision-making—from leaving a church to how we raise our kids—but where we are going requires strategic placement of the wise and Spirit-led. Not every voice gets a vote, and that will make some people mad. Respectfully, let them be angry … boundaries are holy, and wise counsel brings us safety when we're about to walk off a cliff, but not everyone offering us counsel has enough information to give us direction.

Ask the Lord to bring you mentors in seasons of change. Don't isolate yourself or reject godly counsel. But be selective in who speaks into your big decisions, major milestones, and who you share intimate details with regarding the things God is speaking to you.

It's okay if some people don't like your journey. This is between you and God.

> "But Peter and the apostles replied, 'We must obey God rather than any human authority. The God of our ancestors raised Jesus from the dead after you killed him by hanging him on a cross. Then God put him in the place of honor at his right hand as Prince and Savior. He did this so the people of Israel would repent of their sins and be forgiven. We are witnesses of these things and so is the Holy Spirit, who is given by God to those who obey him.'" Acts 5:29–32

Take action: What or who is holding you back from being obedient to what God has called you to do? What is one thing you can do this week to put feet to your faith?

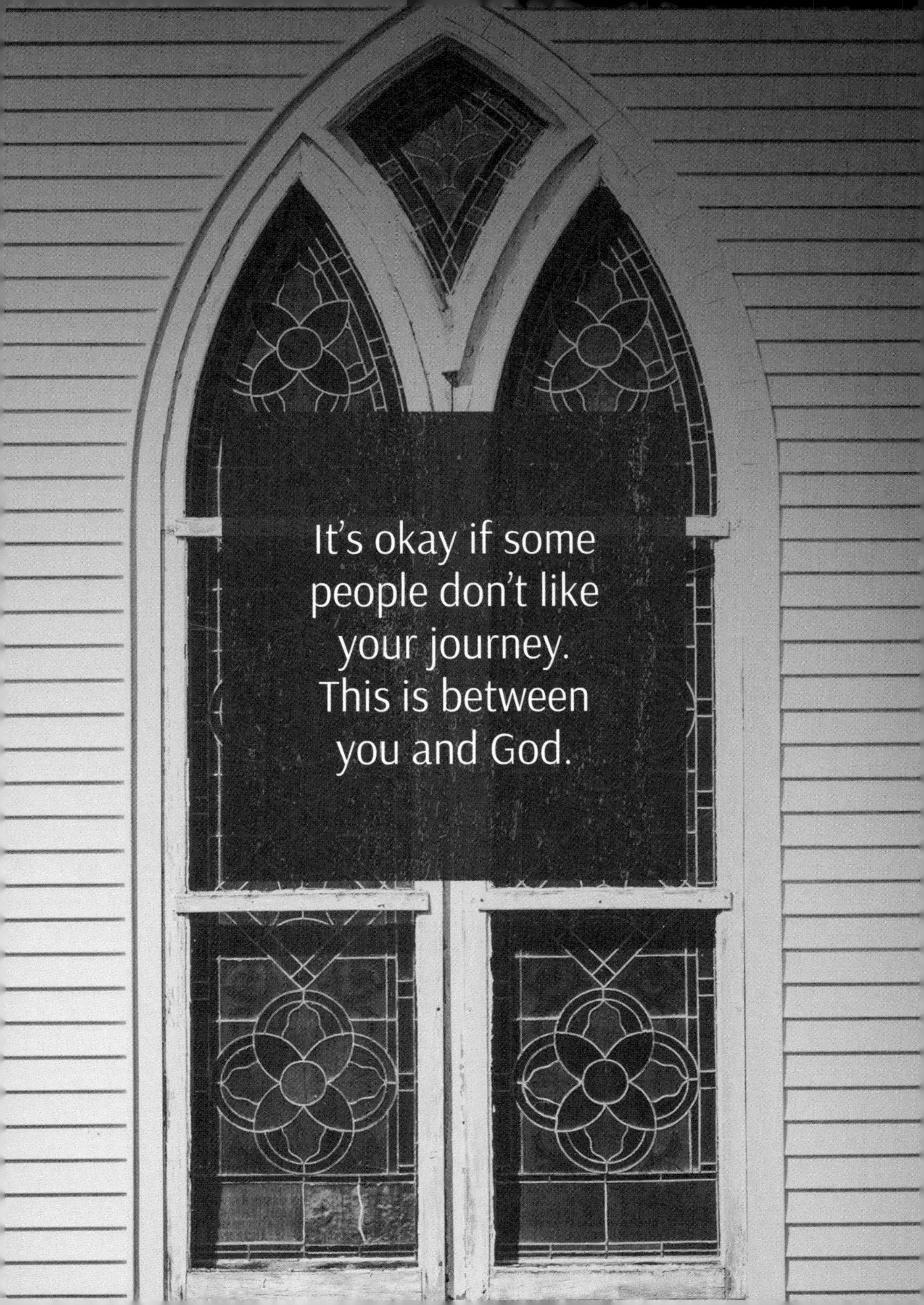
It's okay if some
people don't like
your journey.
This is between
you and God.

CAN you imagine how the disciples felt, their reactions to seeing Jesus for the first time after those three days they believed him to be dead? For three years they were walking with Jesus and learning, serving, gleaning, and then one day they found themselves standing at the foot of the cross watching him bleeding, groaning, dying. Surely a few assumed they would spend their entire lives doing ministry with Jesus, only to end up burying their friend instead.

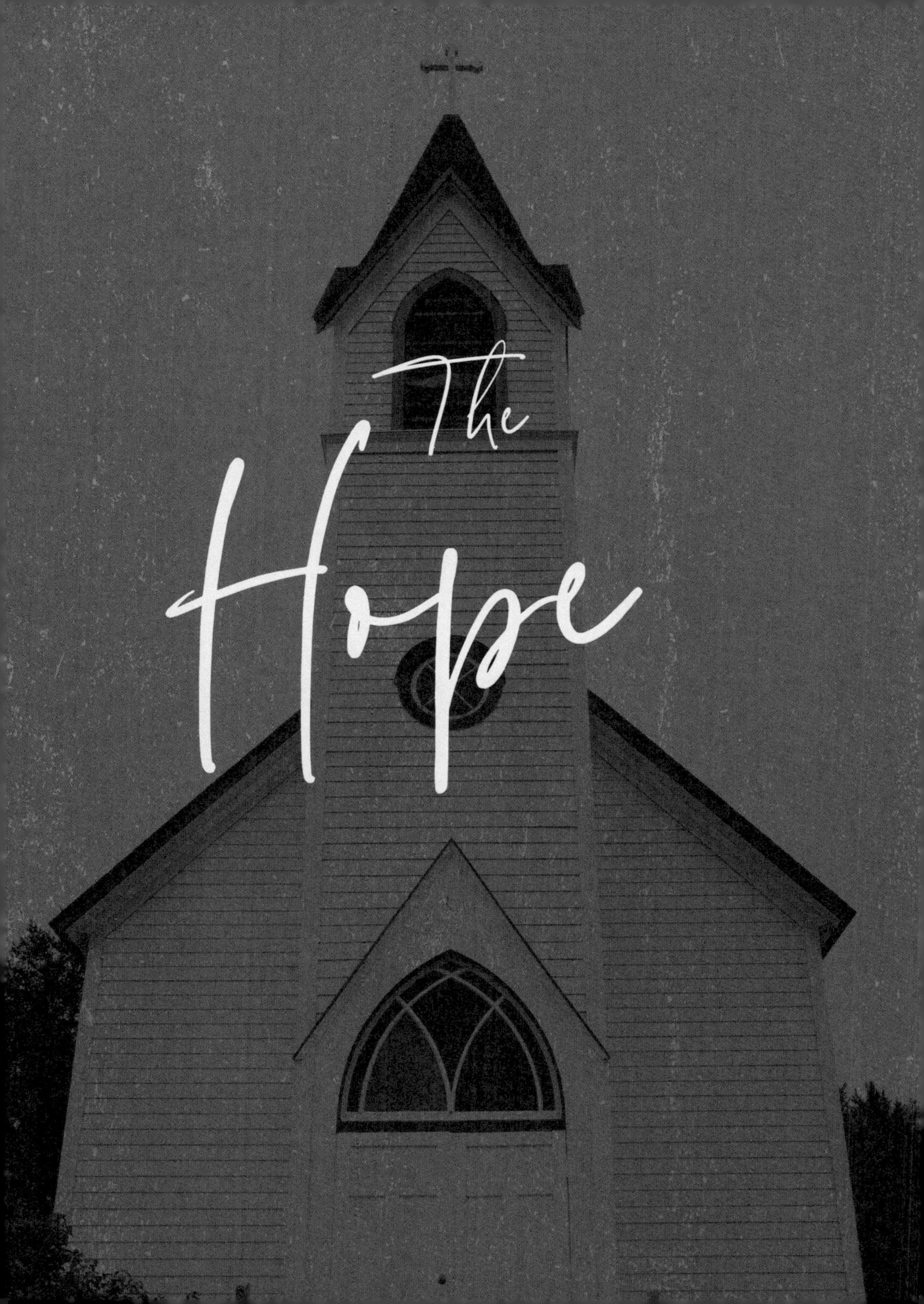
The Hope

In the forty days following his crucifixion and resurrection, Jesus appeared to the apostles at different times, proving to them that he was, in fact, alive. He talked to them about the Kingdom of God and made them a promise that though he had to go on to be with the Father, they would receive power through the Holy Spirit and continue on mission as his witnesses telling people all about him everywhere they went, all the way to the ends of the earth. And just when they thought they might have Jesus a bit longer, he was taken up into a cloud while they watched, until they could no longer see him.

It wasn't long after this that the apostles gathered in a room at the house where they were staying in Jerusalem, along with Mary the mother of Jesus and several other women, and together they

prayed and decided they would continue on mission, going and making disciples. In the second chapter of Acts, the hope of the Holy Spirit fell on the believers who were in the upper room on the day of Pentecost and filled the house where they were all sitting. "And everyone present was filled with the Holy Spirit" (Acts 2:4).

Peter began to prophesy from the prophet Joel, reminding them of the hope that had been promised to them, saying, "'In the last days,' God says, 'I will pour out my Spirit upon all people'" (v. 17). He then reminded them of the powerful miracles, wonders, and signs that had been done through Jesus and that even in the hurt of being betrayed and the hard of taking the cup of wrath, God was faithful to raise him back to life.

We have this same hope.

Peter said, "God raised Jesus from the dead, and we are all witnesses of this. Now he is exalted to the place of highest honor in heaven, at God's right hand. And the Father, as he had promised, gave him the Holy Spirit to pour out upon us, just as you see and hear today" (Acts 2:32–33).

Stayers, God raised Jesus from the dead and he will do the same for you. Just as the Holy Spirit fell on those in the upper room, the Holy Spirit rests upon you now, the beauty in the brutality of the hurt and the glory in the gory of the hard, as we wait in the dark for the light of new life.

It Wasn't Judgment, It Was Discernment

Day 21

WHEN I was ten years old, I went to a birthday party at a local fast-food restaurant where I encountered a man who was bad news. I remember feeling physically ill while the other children laughed and played with him. I was stone cold the entire time, paralyzed by this new feeling that had overtaken me, and it lingered for days to come. I felt badly about it and told my mom, who was quick to help me identify that what I had felt was discernment, not judgment. She told me never to apologize for listening to the Holy Spirit, that even kids could hear him.

Church, we need to use our God-given discernment. We need to use our voices and give voice to the voiceless in situations where others may be in trouble or without someone to advocate for their health and safety. If we see something, we say something and we teach our children to do the same. Discernment is a gift of God available to those who diligently seek him. Pray for discernment so that you, too, may test the spirits and the outside voices screaming over your life!

"My dear friends, don't believe everything you hear. Carefully weigh and examine what people tell you. Not everyone who talks about God comes from God. There are a lot of lying preachers loose in the world. Here's how you test for the genuine Spirit of God. Everyone who confesses openly his faith in Jesus Christ—the Son of God, who came as an actual flesh-and-blood person—comes from God and belongs to God. And everyone who refuses to confess faith in Jesus has nothing in common with God. This is the spirit of antichrist that you heard was coming. Well, here it is, sooner than we thought!" 1 John 4:1–3 (MSG)

Ask for it: Where do you need discernment in your life? Ask God to speak precisely in this situation to bring peace and strategy for all those involved.

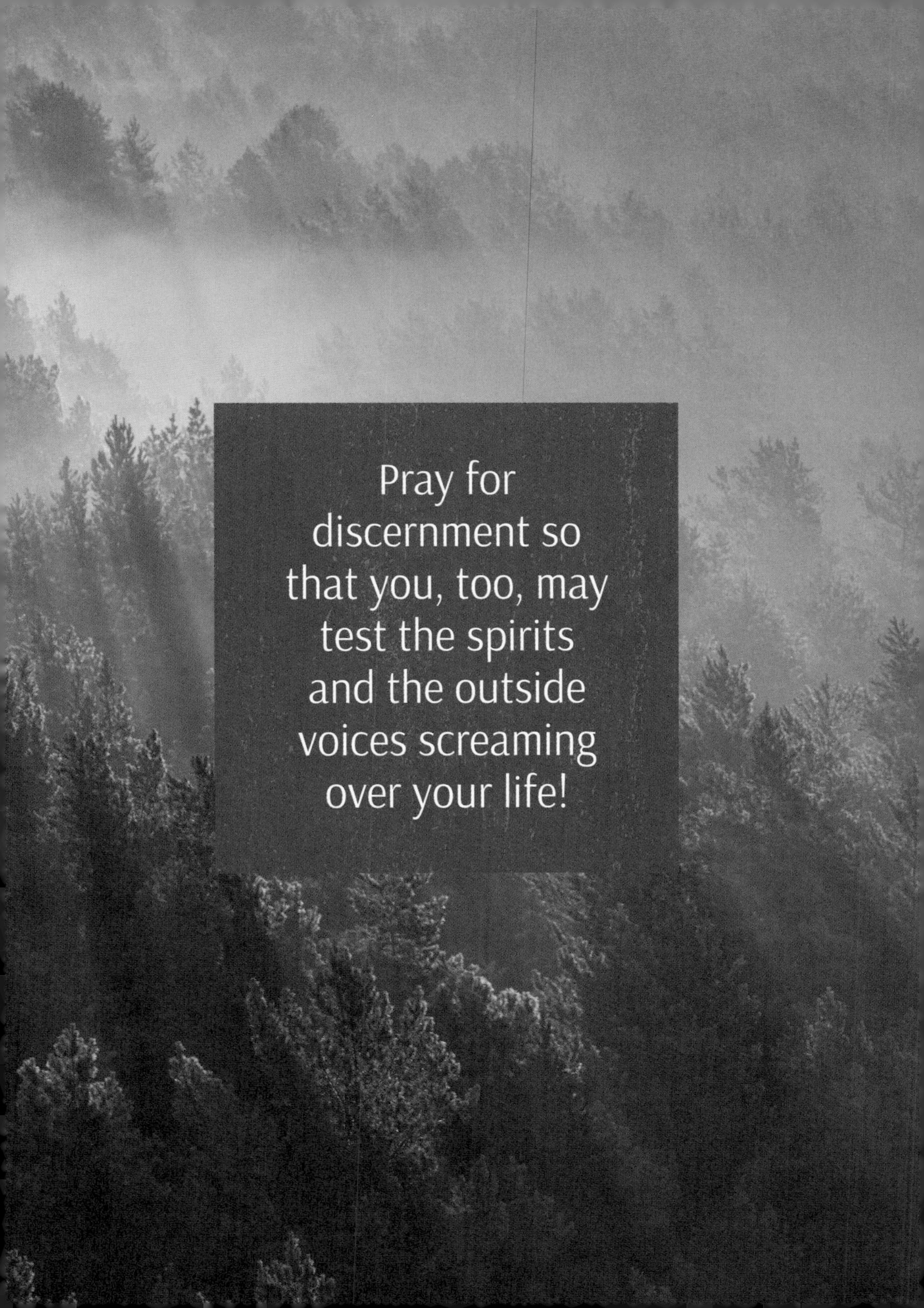
Pray for
discernment so
that you, too, may
test the spirits
and the outside
voices screaming
over your life!

Shine Bright Like a Diamond

Day 22

I ONCE met a young girl at the local gym, and we bonded in the sauna over my fear of getting locked in and her new fear of getting locked in that I had introduced her to. (I'm here to serve you.) We talked for a long time before she found out I was a pastor at a nearby church, and she then shared that she and her sister had been attending recently.

I was so glad Pastor Natalie was the same person in the church as she was in the sauna. Because if I'm honest, that hasn't always been the case. Consistency matters. Our language matters. Our posture matters. Caring for people, loving them, asking questions, truly listening … it all matters. Our jokes, our sobriety, how we speak of others, how we show up on the platform, and off, are a larger picture of Jesus than putting on a fancy suit or leading an hour-long worship service.

Many people will meet Jesus for the first time through you and me long before they step into a church building. That terrifies me. What an honor. What a responsibility. What version of Jesus do they get from me? What version of Jesus do they get from you? Is he kind, patient, slow to anger, and quick to love? Or is he sarcastic, impatient, frustrated, inconsistent, intolerant, or political?

In the past, I've reduced Christ to the popular quarterback and stripped him of his authority and lordship in my attempt to look cool or relevant or woke. Let's be the Jesus we know. But maybe that's part of the problem. Maybe we need to get to know him a little better ourselves. I want to know him. I want to love like him. I want to serve like him. I want people to know that Jesus. Jesus, show us who you are.

Many people will meet Jesus through you and me before they will ever step foot into a church.

Shine bright.

Stay salty.

Don't embarrass the family.

"You are the salt of the earth. But what good is salt if it has lost its flavor? Can you make it salty again? It will be thrown out and trampled underfoot as worthless. You are the light of the world—like a city on a hilltop that cannot be hidden. No one lights a lamp and then puts it under a basket. Instead, a lamp is placed on a stand, where it gives light to everyone in the house. In the same way, let your good deeds shine out for all to see, so that everyone will praise your heavenly Father." Matthew 5:13–16

Shine on: How have you been salt and light to those around you? Do you reflect the hope of Christ wherever you go, or have you felt dim and a little bitter?

Shine bright.
Stay salty.
Don't embarrass the family.

A Platform Is a Pricey Privilege

Day 23

WHEN I was a little girl, microphones weren't just handed out. Mics had brightly covered sponge covers, were hidden in a box under the pulpit, and everyone knew which color belonged to whom. My favorite was the red one. And every Sunday those mics were handed out to the singers and preachers who had been trusted to use their voices with the understanding that the guys in the sound booth could cut them off at any time.

Every Sunday morning someone would be asked to testify and one of those precious mics would be handed to a saint, who would take their place on the platform and share what the Lord had done in their life. Voice trembling, hands shaking, eyes closed as if they knew the weight of that moment. The price of that platform.

We would lean in to listen in a holy hush because we knew microphones weren't just given out; these voices had been tested. Tried. Proven. Edited by a lifetime of accountability, time in the Word, and in the presence of God.

I'm afraid that because of social media, we've forgotten the influence, the cost of a platform. That when much is given, much is required, and we no longer feel the impact of our words. We just want to be heard. I'm watching our desire to be heard and validated become more important than our desire to love and seek to understand, and we don't tremble under the weight anymore.

We all want the platform without the price, but with every unmeasured word we are losing connection with those who have been watching our lives. We aren't holding the mic with gratitude that we get to use our voice, rather we're grabbing it and demanding that people listen. So many voices have been given access to our lives that we can't hear the wise ones who still humbly speak with that holy hush.

Sometimes the wisest voices are the quietest. We want to use our voices to speak life with fear and trembling in the Lord. Like those dear saints, we want

to hold the mic with our voices trembling, hands shaking, and eyes closed. May we all know the price of our platform. Let's make Kingdom deposits and eternal investments with every post and story.

I'll even give you the red mic.

> "Don't be misled—you cannot mock the justice of God. You will always harvest what you plant. Those who live only to satisfy their own sinful nature will harvest decay and death from that sinful nature. But those who live to please the Spirit will harvest everlasting life from the Spirit. So let's not get tired of doing what is good. At just the right time we will reap a harvest of blessing if we don't give up. Therefore, whenever we have the opportunity, we should do good to everyone—especially to those in the family of faith." Galatians 6:7–10

Steward it: How have you used your influence, platform, or voice recently? Are you bringing peace or panic?

May we all know the price of our platform. Let's make Kingdom deposits and eternal investments with every post and story.

There Are More People for You Than Against You

Day 24

I AM speaking to the child inside of us who has their fists curled and brow furrowed, ready for the next fight. That orphan spirit will make us think the whole world is out to see us fail when we have all of heaven cheering us on …

Be careful not to grow bitter in your attempt to be better. Some may hope to watch us fall, but God raises us up every single time and there are more watching you get up. There are more inspired by your staying. Anyone can take their toys and go home, but to remain in the yard and finish the game among jeers is commendable, and soon they'll be drowned out by cheers.

There are more people who love you than hate you. More people who hope you succeed than who hope you fail. There are more good people than bad. There is more hope than despair. You have a message and a ministry, and while it's true that some might quietly hope you don't make it, there are more praying you through. But first you have to unclench those fists and relax that lower lip so people can actually hear what you have to say.

You have an angel army and family of God around you … get up.

> "Therefore, since we are surrounded by such a huge crowd of witnesses to the life of faith, let us strip off every weight that slows us down, especially the sin that so easily trips us up. And let us run with endurance the race God has set before us." Hebrews 12:1

Gratitude: Who are the ones who have cheered you on through difficult seasons? Who do you know who could use some words of encouragement from you?

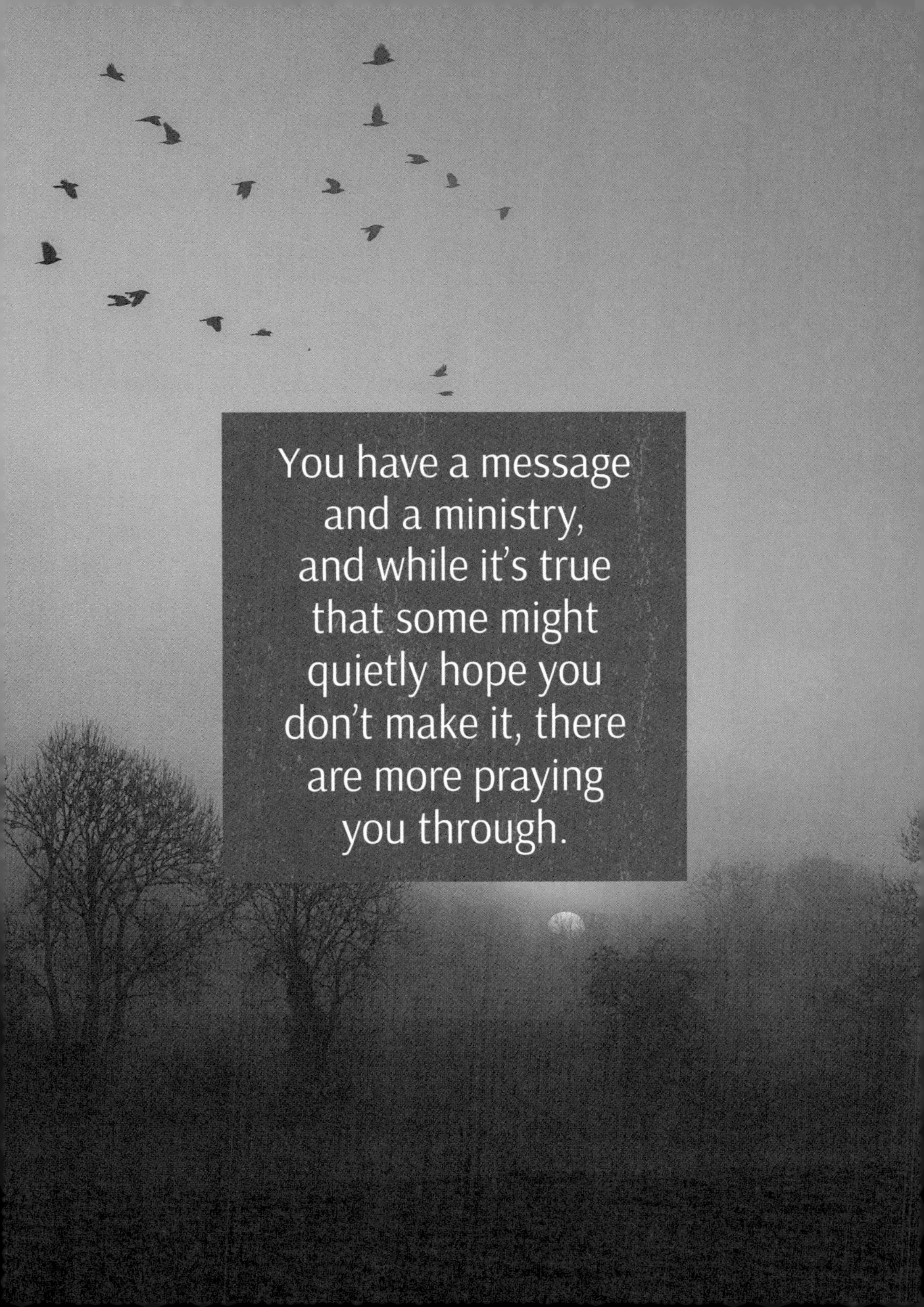
You have a message
and a ministry,
and while it's true
that some might
quietly hope you
don't make it, there
are more praying
you through.

Jesus Did It

Day 25

NEVER kick down a door to a room you think you belong in. Let God make the introductions and opportunities. That way, when people ask how you got where you are, the only answer is "Jesus."

You aren't left out, left behind, forgotten, unwanted. You aren't the least talented. You aren't second string. You aren't the last resort or backup. Somewhere there is a room and inside it is a table with your name on it where a very specific group of people, who God placed strategically, will be part of your journey for his glory and your good.

What we think we deserve is often in conflict with what God desires for us, and his timing and location, even the assignment, are rarely in alignment with our own. We will peer into windows of other rooms and see people sitting where we want to sit, doing what we want to do, and it will give us FOMO that will either make us desperate or despondent—both are disobedience. We can see it as a missed turn or as an opportunity to grow, as protection from the

Lord or rejection by people. How we behave in the seasons of "not yet" speaks to how we will steward what is coming.

Remember: If God isn't in it, you don't want it. And if he isn't where you're headed, you don't want to go. Because there will be a day when the rooms are rattled and the tables flipped, and you'll need every ounce of the Holy Spirit to remain in position in the shaking. Don't demand from people what God isn't ready to give you. Every open door isn't God; every closed door isn't rejection. You'll need discernment that only comes with growing in Christ and obedience to follow his voice and not your own.

Because when he finally opens that door, it will be to give him glory and make him known. And he needs to know you will give credit where credit is due.

> "Every time I think of you, I give thanks to my God. Whenever I pray, I make my requests for all of you with joy, for you have been my partners in spreading the Good News about Christ from the time you first heard it until now. And I am certain that God, who began the good work within you, will continue his work until it is finally finished on the day when Christ Jesus returns." Philippians 1:3–6

Test it: Write down some opportunities you've prayed for but aren't sure they're from God. Ask him for wisdom and wise counsel to discern the truth.

Don't demand from people what God isn't ready to give you. Every open door isn't God; every closed door isn't rejection.

You Can't Expire

Day 26

I'LL be the first to admit, I spent most of my thirties fearing I would "age out" in ministry, especially as a woman. Can I be brutally honest? If you're only in ministry to be the face of a program, project, or album cover, you'll be a one-hit wonder. Jesus didn't put that flame in you so it could burn out; he says we have to fan it. Steward it. Speak life over it. Protect it. I'm watching our flames get blown out one by one because we didn't count on a calling that doesn't expire—but it does evolve.

Sometimes evolution looks like the end of an era, when really, it's the beginning of the real reason God put us on this earth. Some of us would rather be told we're too old than stay and wrestle through a new assignment. Many have assumed it's easier to quit than to teach old dogs new tricks.

But I have news for the old dogs. The only way you can age out of your calling is if you opt out. Quit. Give up. The enemy is counting on it. He doesn't want seasoned mothers and fathers in the faith sticking around to raise up this next generation; he knows he'll never get to them if he has to go through us.

You are not too old. You don't need to be relevant, you need to be resilient. Unshakable. Immovable. Unoffendable. You are just beginning. You woke up this morning with air in your lungs and a mission of the Great Commission written on your heart, so put on your skinny jeans and get on your way.

God isn't finished with you yet. God's calling doesn't expire. His mandates never grow stale. When he speaks, even dry bones get up and create an army. You're evolving, and God still has so much planned for you.

You can't age out of what God has called you to do. Your assignment may evolve, but you don't expire.

> "Listen to me, descendants of Jacob, all you who remain in Israel. I have cared for you since you were born. Yes, I carried you before you were born. I will be your God throughout your lifetime—until your hair is white with age. I made you, and I will care for you. I will carry you along and save you." Isaiah 46:3–4

New era: Write out the biggest God dream you've had that feels impossible and give it to him. You never know where it will go, even if you feel too young or too old.

You can't age out of what God has called you to do. Your assignment may evolve, but you don't expire.

Ministry Is Brutiful (Brutal and Beautiful)

Day 27

SPOILER alert: Ministry is messy. The church isn't perfect. We're all a little crazy. God is really good. You are ridiculously loved.

Forgive me if I've made any of this look easy. Because the truth is, ministry is both brutal and beautiful and I'd rather focus on the beauty. But in every paradise there is a serpent asking, "Did God really say that?" And even on the most beautiful, breathtaking mornings we are tempted to listen to him. We need to talk about the hard stuff, the truth that sometimes God's will for our lives makes us weep, throw tantrums, and mourn what has been lost. My will and his will are in a constant war, and my wants and desires often pull me away from the Garden gate. He's calling for me, and I'm going the opposite direction.

Don't tell me things I don't want to hear. Don't ask that of me. Don't take this from me.

Forgive me for … hiding my sleepless nights. For posting smiling selfies and group shots filled with laughter when my insides were falling apart. For cheerleading from the sidelines when I'm ready to quit the game.

Maybe if we start getting honest, we'll realize we're all in the same battle. Not alone. Not crazy. That this struggle is real, but our God saves and is fighting for us on our most war-weary days. And that we have each other, this army. We don't have to quit. White flags aren't bad, it just means we need a little help.

I have no idea how to do any of this well. If I'm doing it right. If I'm even on track. I just know that I can't quit, and trust me, I've wanted to. Nearly every single day. So, I'll commit to you that I'm finishing this, but I'm also going to be honest when I don't want to. Please, do the same. This isn't supposed to be easy; it's going to be messy, but it's what leads us back to Jesus every single time. Keep showing up. Don't ever stop showing up.

> "But you should keep a clear mind in every situation. Don't be afraid of suffering for the Lord. Work at telling others the Good News, and fully carry out the ministry God has given you. As for me, my life has already been poured out as an offering to God. The time of my death is near. I have fought the good fight, I have finished the race, and I have remained faithful. And now the prize awaits me—the crown of righteousness, which the Lord, the righteous Judge, will give me on the day of his return. And the prize is not just for me but for all who eagerly look forward to his appearing." 2 Timothy 4:5–8

Embrace it: What "brutiful" season are you in now?
How have you seen God show up?
What are you praying will come from it?

Keep showing up.
Don’t ever stop
showing up.

Go to Church Even When You're Not in Charge

Day 28

MY husband was a professional pitcher for fifteen years, and when we first started dating, I asked him if he enjoyed attending baseball games. He said, "Sometimes, but other times it's like I'm watching my friends work." I could relate. My whole life had been a series of waiting for Sunday, revivals, camp meetings, and assemblies where we all had assignments. Church was my job and Sunday was game day.

Visiting a church while away on vacation or anywhere we weren't in charge felt like showing up on game day to watch my friends work. I didn't know how to sit in a pew and not assess, assign, critique … As I got older and had seasons where I wasn't on a church staff, I couldn't worship, I couldn't focus, and that's when I realized how fragile my faith had become.

Did I even know Jesus as anyone other than my boss? Did I see the church staff as colaborers or my coworkers? Did I love the church as my brothers and sisters or see them as consumers? It's easy to show up and work, be productive, prove our worth, make decisions, feel important … to spend service time talking to other staff people in the lobby and green room.

But sometimes God gives us time in his house not to clean, assign chores, do the grilling or cooking but to simply sit in the living room and be ministered to. By his family, in his presence, without a single task at hand.

And we don't sit there writing down ways we could do it better. We're not evaluating the house or its people. We're just there to encounter the Father, and we've got to get better at it. Learning when we're not the teacher. Worshipping when we're not the leader. Showing up even when nobody is looking for us.

It's what keeps us falling in love with Jesus. What sharpens our faith. Because some of our greatest ministry will happen in conversations in parking lots, between stalls in a bathroom, picking up our kids from children's ministry simply as a fellow believer. Let's keep showing up to the House of God even when it's not ours to manage, because we're desperate for him. Better is one day in his house than anywhere else.

> "But the time is coming—indeed it's here now—when true worshipers will worship the Father in spirit and in truth. The Father is looking for those who will worship him that way. For God is Spirit, so those who worship him must worship in spirit and in truth." John 4:23–24

Own it: Get creative! Who can you bring alongside you to be the hands of Jesus from the church foyer to your school, workplace, or neighborhood?

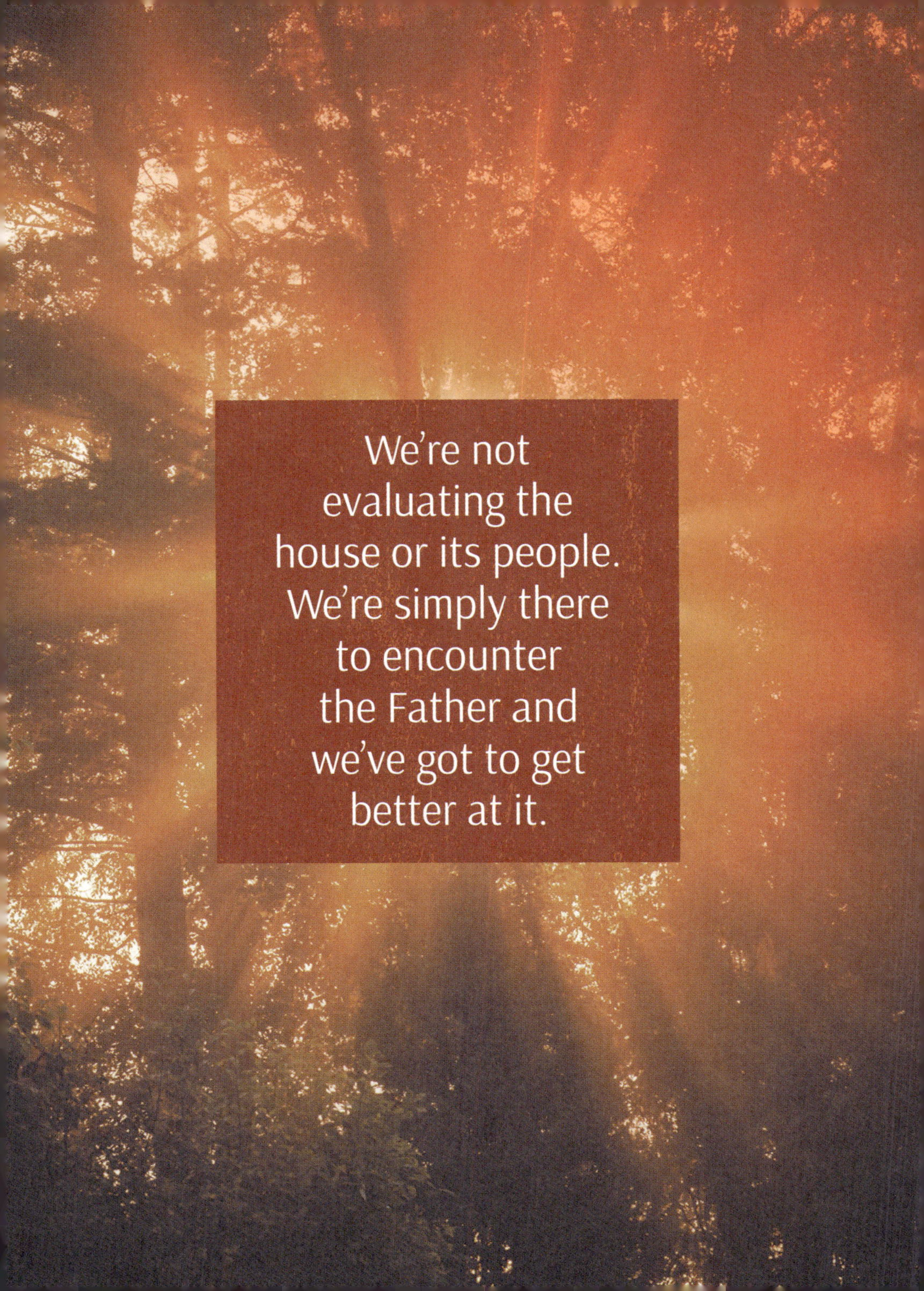
We're not evaluating the house or its people. We're simply there to encounter the Father and we've got to get better at it.

Our God Provides

Day 29

SELF-preservation is not a fruit of the Spirit.

Our bodies are hardwired to self-preserve, for fight or flight. Should we encounter a bear on an empty trail or find ourselves at gunpoint in an empty parking garage, if we are physically and emotionally healthy people, we will feel our survival instincts kick in to pull out bear spray or scream for help to save ourselves.

How often we forget our worldly tactics don't work in the Kingdom of God, where we actually lose our lives to save our lives. And as people who often run—from pain, rejection, and correction—this following-Jesus thing is already a hard sell.

But self-preservation isn't a fruit of the Spirit. Spraying each other in the eye because we feel attacked by not getting the solo, the position, or a pat on the back from our pastors or peers isn't how we should do things.

God gave us gifts and callings and established authority before we took our first breaths, so stop holding your breath; what he has for you is coming.

He has a place with your name on it at his table that was set before you ever learned how to use silverware; stop stealing food from your siblings. Children of God aren't beggars, nor are we scavengers. Pull your claws in, there's enough for everyone.

When we get scared, overwhelmed, when we feel left out or unseen or devalued or replaced, this is our strategy: Lead with love, serve with joy, live peacefully, practice patience, show kindness, offer generosity, war with faithfulness, demonstrate gentleness, operate in self-control.

Jesus could have hidden in the garden or chopped off the guard's other ear. But he didn't. Instead, though blameless, he submitted to the process of a sinner's death and chose to heal others rather than fight back.

This is our Jesus. Who teaches us that laying down our lives leads to a resurrection.

> "But the Holy Spirit produces this kind of fruit in our lives: love, joy, peace, patience, kindness, goodness, faithfulness, gentleness, and self-control. There is no law against these things! Those who belong to Christ Jesus have nailed the passions and desires of their sinful nature to his cross and crucified them there. Since we are living by the Spirit, let us follow the Spirit's leading in every part of our lives. Let us not become conceited, or provoke one another, or be jealous of one another." Galatians 5:22–26

Provision: What does surrender look like for you to fully trust God will provide and meet every need according to his riches and glory?

God gave us gifts and callings and established authority before we took our first breaths, so stop holding your breath; what he has for you is coming.

Just Get Me to Jesus

Day 30

WE all want friends who will lower us through a roof to our healing, who will worship with us through our midnight hour, friends who will run to Jesus on our behalf who will call us out of an early grave.

We all want an upper room community who isn't afraid of a little fire, who knows how to fan a flame and stir up a gift. Intercessors who go to war without ceasing and worshippers who go into battle as warriors. We want a church who knows the Word of God and wields it like a double-edged sword, for it is burning in their bellies and burning in their bones. We want an army who knows how to fight and a family who knows how to love.

There will be counterfeit communities who will promise you solidarity but leave you in solitude. They will promise healing only to lick your wounds for their saltiness. They will offer sweet revenge but it's a cup of bitterness. Misery loves company. Don't pull up a chair until you know who is around the table. Be wise where you sit, aware of who invited you, and discern if you'll be pulled down to a lower standard or called up to a higher purpose.

We can be the friends who break through the roof for each other. I pray we never stop looking for ways to lead others to Jesus.

> "Some men took a man who was not able to move his body to Jesus. He was carried on a bed. They looked for a way to take the man into the house where Jesus was. But they could not find a way to take him in because of so many people. They made a hole in the roof over where Jesus stood. Then they let the bed with the sick man on it down before Jesus. When Jesus saw their faith, He said to the man, 'Friend, your sins are forgiven.'" Luke 5:18–20 (NLV)

Community: What has biblical community looked like throughout your life? How can you help create Christ-like community in your home even in busy seasons?

We can be the friends who break through the roof for each other. I pray we never stop looking for ways to lead others to Jesus.

CAN you imagine being in the upper room as the Holy Spirit rested upon each believer? The power of the wind, the warmth of those flames, the presence of God visible and tangible for the very first time beheld by human eyes.

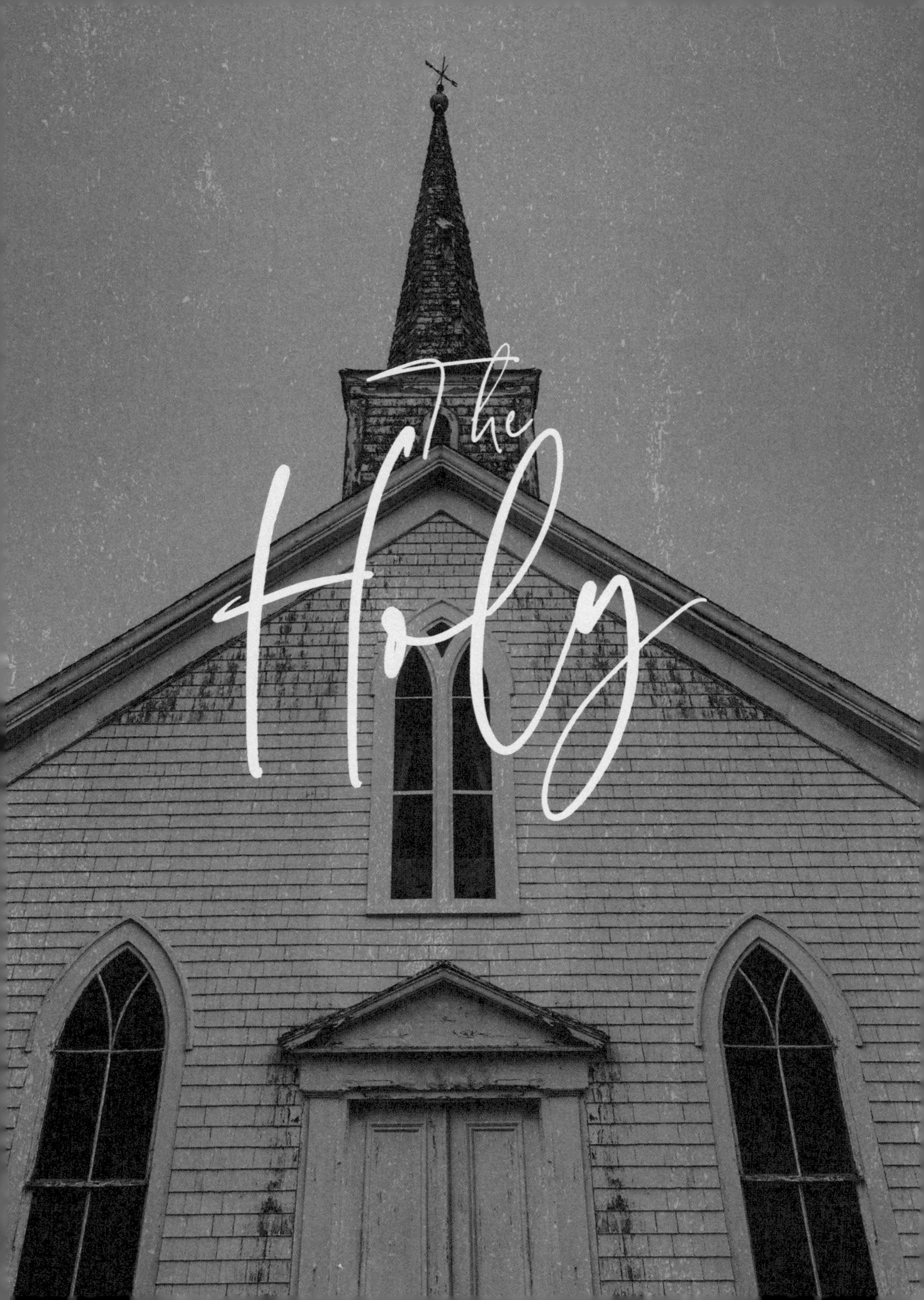
The Holy

I don't think it's by accident that Peter, the one who nearly drowned because he didn't lock eyes with Jesus ... Peter, the one who denied Jesus three times ... Peter, the one who cut off the guard's ear in the garden ... was the one who stood in the upper room that day and preached perhaps the very first sermon to the very first church. He was bold, precise, Spirit-filled, and Spirit-led, reminding us all that you don't have to be perfect to be used by God, but you have to be willing to remain through the hurt and the hard to get to the hope and the holy.

God will use your failures, doubts, and weaknesses to reveal his glory and power to a world looking into the windows of our upper rooms for hope.

In Acts chapter 2 verse 41 we read, "Those who believed what Peter said were baptized and added to the church that day—about 3,000 in all."

Why do we go through the hurt and the hard and believe for the hope we have been promised? Because the holy isn't just for us, it's for everyone looking for a Savior, and we are part of God's plan to preach salvation and hope to a lost world. It's here we can say these words Paul spoke in Philippians and actually mean them: "Yes, everything else is worthless when compared with the infinite value of knowing Christ Jesus my Lord. For his sake I have discarded everything else, counting it all as garbage, so that I could gain Christ and become one with him" (3:8–9).

It is in our brokenness that the holiness of God shines through us like stained-glass windows, individually and corporately, where we finally see the whole picture. A remnant of those hurt, who have walked through the hard to tell a story of the hope and the holy that comes with remaining. Tarrying.

Staying.

Paul went on to say, "I no longer count on my own righteousness through obeying the law; rather, I become righteous through faith in Christ.... I want to know Christ and experience the mighty power that raised him from the dead. I want to suffer with him, sharing in his death, so that one way or another I will experience the resurrection from the dead!" (Philippians 3:9–11).

We have been crucified and raised with Christ.

He was hurt (betrayed), he endured the hard (those three days between crucifixion and resurrection), he gave us hope (resurrection), and now we stand in the holy (the mission to take the message of Jesus out through the power of the Holy Spirit) because that is what our God does.

Our God finishes what he starts.

And that includes the work in you and in me.

Sit with Sages

Day 31

IF we only follow the famous, we miss out on learning from the faithful.

I understand what many of us struggle with: We're on social media and we see Christian influencers in rooms, on shows promoting projects and books, at churches, in selfies with certain people, and we think, *How did they get there? Why them and not me? I wish I was friends with* _________.

I know because I was there for most of my late twenties and thirties and it's an awful feeling to want something we were never meant to have, or desire, and even if we got it, we all know it wouldn't be enough. Longing for fame only prolonged the process on the journey to my God-assigned ministry. Longing for visibility only revealed my need to remain hidden; I wasn't ready to carry the weight of the cross with my ego taking up so much space.

If you're blessed to get to do this ministry thing, surround yourself with the faithful saints who wear crowns of silver and laugh lines from joy that has replaced mourning. Go where your yes takes you, big or small, seen or unseen, and love people until you get back on the plane or in the car, exhausted from it all.

Can the faithful be famous? Sure. But that isn't our goal; Jesus is the prize. If you want longevity in this ministry life, live among the faithful.

> "Timothy, I thank God for you—the God I serve with a clear conscience, just as my ancestors did. Night and day I constantly remember you in my prayers. I long to see you again, for I remember your tears as we parted. And I will be filled with joy when we are together again. I remember your genuine faith, for you share the faith that first filled your grandmother Lois and your mother, Eunice. And I know that same faith continues strong in you. This is why I remind you to fan into flames the spiritual gift God gave you when I laid my hands on you. For God has not given us a spirit of fear and timidity, but of power, love, and self-discipline." 2 Timothy 1:3–7

Seek it out: We were never meant to do this life alone. Who are some sages you could learn from? How can you be a Paul to a Timothy in your life?

If you want longevity in this ministry life, live among the faithful.

Stay with It

Day 32

IF you're still here holding on to Jesus and loving his Church, I know it hasn't been an easy road. It's brave to stay. Holy to hide in the cleft of the rock. Honest to admit you have thick skin and a soft heart. Sometimes it means going. None of us are still here by our own strength, rather a bold bravery that can only come from trusting the promises and Word of God. Stay on the vine, don't let go. Abide just a little longer. For the joy set before you, eyes on Jesus.

How brave it is to stay.

> "Staying with it—that's what God requires. Stay with it to the end. You won't be sorry, and you'll be saved. All during this time, the good news—the Message of the kingdom—will be preached all over the world, a witness staked out in every country. And then the end will come." Matthew 24:13–14 (MSG)

Stick it out: In what ways have you wanted to "quit" lately? Maybe not physically but mentally check out. Ask God to reignite old flames or provide fresh vision.

Abide just a little longer. For the joy set before you, eyes on Jesus.
How brave it is to stay.

It Is Holy to Heal

Day 33

I SEE you healing, gathering up the brokenness as God prepares to make a masterpiece out of the mess …

I see you getting out of bed when you'd rather cover your head. I hear you praying a line or two with lingering hope in your weary voice when it has felt like God is silent. I'm watching you hug the necks of those who stabbed you in the back and speak life about those who nearly killed you. Forgiveness is so becoming on you; wear it like a fine perfume. Others see it too, the Great Healer doing a deep work in you and on you. Those scars aren't scary, they are holy. Wear them honestly. Bare them boldly.

The next great revival in God's Church won't be led by those who have never been wounded, rather by those with limps and lumps who have refused to give up. And God sees you here too. Sowing seed when you'd rather be buried, going when you'd prefer to leave, and choosing reconciliation over revenge. This healing journey is not for the faint of heart. You aren't alone, we're all being pieced back together and patched up as we run. Rest when you can, but keep your eyes on the finish line. Don't get distracted. Don't get discouraged. God does good work in our brokenness and makes his power known in our healing.

Did you know God is capable of healing us all? From hurt, offense, whatever category you find yourself in, you aren't too broken or scarred for him. He does his best triage on those of us willing to confess our brokenness, and he knows how to carry those of us too weary to run. I know it's hard to show up, to keep going, to stay. I see you trying. I see you healing. God sees it too. And it's beautiful, even in the brutality of the reality. His grace shines through your broken pieces, his presence glows through your tears. Tell your story of heartbreak now; one day it will be a testimony of redemption.

> "For God called you to do good, even if it means suffering, just as Christ suffered for you. He is your example, and you must follow in his steps. He never sinned, nor ever deceived anyone. He did not retaliate when he was insulted, nor threaten revenge when he suffered. He left his case in the hands of God, who always judges fairly. He personally carried our sins in his body on the cross so that we can be dead to sin and live for what is right. By his wounds you are healed. Once you were like sheep who wandered away. But now you have turned to your Shepherd, the Guardian of your souls." 1 Peter 2:21–25

The ministry of healing:

How are you healing in this season? Celebrate the small steps you're taking toward finding God in the process.

Tell your story of
heartbreak now;
one day it will
be a testimony
of redemption.

Shine Bright

Day 34

AS disciples of Jesus Christ, we carry the Holy Spirit. We walk and talk with something different through the corridors of this world, and we know we're set apart. We are glowing with the presence of God, and people can't help but take notice. I know there are days we wish we could just blend in, but it's not who we were created to be.

Let's show up every day with confidence in our Creator that he made us just right. He made us for such a time as this. He made us to carry what nobody else can carry. Don't hide your light under a bush, shine bright and bold and brazen! You aren't a spectacle, you aren't too much, and this world needs your sparkle. They need every bit of your joy and laughter and encouragement on days that feel dark and overwhelming.

The presence of God looks good on you!

Shine on.

"When Moses came down from Mount Sinai with the two tablets of the covenant law in his hands, he was not aware that his face was radiant because he had spoken with the Lord." Exodus 34:29 (NIV)

Show it off: Are you spending time daily with God, talking to him and worshipping? Where do you see God in your life, and how are you showing him to others?

The presence of God looks good on you!
Shine on.

Shake It Off

Day 35

DON'T take old dirt into new seasons.

Part of growing up is learning when to uproot and move on, kicking the dust off our feet and going out of obedience. One reason we struggle with fully healing from what happened to us in one season of barren soil is our inability to move on without carrying some of the old soil with us. The worst thing we can do is carry tainted dirt into fresh gardens, but we do it because it's familiar and it's been stuck to our shoe for so long that it's become part of our stride.

Church hurt isn't a death sentence, though it will stunt our growth. It isn't our ending, but it does make it hard for fresh beginnings. God promises to do a new thing; he offers us new mercies every single day, but it's hard to receive the new when we can't shake off the old.

I am praying that as we step into the holy, the Holy Spirit will teach us to kick the dust off our feet from years of rejection and fear so we can step into fresh starts with his presence and peace. Let's take the lessons we have learned and the good memories but leave the rest behind. God was there and he is with us now. We don't have to quit to start over. We trust God got us out before we withered and that's because we might be pressed but we're never crushed. He is the kind of Father who only buries us to bring forth a resurrection. It's a new season.

> "Don't take any money in your money belts—no gold, silver, or even copper coins. Don't carry a traveler's bag with a change of clothes and sandals or even a walking stick. Don't hesitate to accept hospitality, because those who work deserve to be fed. Whenever you enter a city or village, search for a worthy person and stay in his home until you leave town. When you enter the home, give it your blessing. If it turns out to be a worthy home, let your blessing stand; if it is not, take back the blessing. If any household or town refuses to welcome you or listen to your message, shake its dust from your feet as you leave." Matthew 10:9–14

Shake it off: What are some old habits or hurts you're still carrying? What do you need to let go of to grab hold of the new that God is inviting you into now?

He is the kind of Father who only buries us to bring forth a resurrection. It's a new season.

Battle Ready

Day 36

IF you've been treating the church like a country club, now would be a good time to show up like it's a training ground.

I like coffee as much as any Gen X worship leader, and after growing up in churches with fewer than three hundred people, I appreciate things like air-conditioning, fancy accommodations, and paved parking lots. But some of us are getting really comfortable and we're losing reverence for the House of God. It shows in how we speak of her leaders and people as if they work for us. We've become consumers with quick fingers behind anonymous screen names to rate sermons like we're rating Airbnbs.

Church, now is not the time. If we aren't walking into every gathering of believers like we're walking onto a training field next to fellow soldiers fighting against the same enemy, we've already lost the battle. If we can't respect our leadership and don't view our pastors as generals with God-given strategy to take us fearlessly into the Word and Presence of God, but have reduced them to entertainers who put on a show to be critiqued, let this be a reminder to us all:

The church is a dwelling place for the Spirit of God (Ephesians 2:20–22).

God's temple is holy, and we are that temple (1 Corinthians 3:17).

We are called to equip, not complain or compare or compete (Ephesians 4:12).

There is a world looking to us for a Living Hope in a life of despair, and where there is unity, God commands his blessing … we can't give up. We can't grow weary in doing good. I pray we walk into our churches on mission more concerned with the new face or new family than the sound of the music or temperature of the coffee. Love God. Love people. This is our mission.

> "You are fellow citizens with the saints and members of the household of God, built on the foundation of the apostles and prophets, Christ Jesus himself being the cornerstone, in whom the whole structure, being joined together, grows into a holy temple in the Lord." Ephesians 2:19–21 (ESV)

Armor up: How can you be battle ready so the enemy doesn't use old tactics to take you down? What are some weak areas you need to work on? Where are you feeling strong?

Love God. Love people. This is our mission.

The Good Sheep

Day 37

WHEN working on my first round of edits for one of my books, my editor called me concerned I wasn't fully healed from some things, and she was right. I was bleeding out all over my readers, and perhaps that would sell books because everyone loves a victim, they either give us someone to cheer for or they make us feel better that we're not alone in our misery. As I healed, my writing turned a corner to a more honest yet honoring space. I also started writing songs and remembering who I was in Christ apart from the things that had happened to me.

Yes, pastors and leaders need to lead us as the church into healthy culture and many of us feel powerless and voiceless, but we're not. We can report abuse and the things hurting God's sheep by using our voices to help those who have been hurt to heal. There are more sheep who long to see our churches safe and healthy than there are corrupt shepherds. I promise you that. I believe there is a radical remnant rising up, and we will have to stop telling our sob stories on repeat and start speaking to who we are becoming as a healed people ready to see change. I include myself in this, we are in this together.

It's true, the church has been messy, but there is more good than bad and it's time we start talking about the blessings and miracles. The church isn't perfect, but neither are we.

Are we ready to stop blaming the church and start being the Church?

> "Is there any encouragement from belonging to Christ? Any comfort from his love? Any fellowship together in the Spirit? Are your hearts tender and compassionate? Then make me truly happy by agreeing wholeheartedly with each other, loving one another, and working together with one mind and purpose. Don't be selfish; don't try to impress others. Be humble, thinking of others as better than yourselves. Don't look out only for your own interests, but take an interest in others, too. You must have the same attitude that Christ Jesus had." Philippians 2:1–5

Rise up: Many people have been hurt by the church and are looking for hope. How can your story introduce them to a whole and healed church?

It's true, the church has been messy, but there is more good than bad and it's time we start talking about the blessings and miracles.

When I Want to Quit, I Will Remember ...

Day 38

GOD has given me a specific assignment and he has equipped me with every tool I will need to fulfill his purpose and complete the work he began in me. Nobody can stop the power of God from moving in my life. If I am willing, he is able to fulfill every word and promise he has spoken over me and will work through me to see his Kingdom come. Even in my death he will be made known. I'm not the only one who is tired or afraid, God has given me a Kingdom family to run beside me and good soil we labor on together. I am not alone.

Resting is not quitting. I can take a nap and trust my God-given assignment will be waiting for me when I wake up. God will not punish me for taking time to heal. I don't lose commission or my position when I ask for help, I won't be replaced in the family of God. There are many times I simply need to be with God instead of doing for God. He delights in my friendship more than my performance. I believe in the message he has entrusted to me and the mission to go and make disciples. God has given me freedom to deliver the Gospel through the unique gifts he has given me. I am wanted and accepted in the family of God and have a seat prepared at the table just for me. I add value, passion, experience, and God-given characteristics that build the Church and strengthen the body of Christ.

God has never given up on me. I will not give up on him.

> "It seems to me that God has put us who bear his Message on stage in a theater in which no one wants to buy a ticket. We're something everyone stands around and stares at, like an accident in the street. We're the Messiah's misfits. You might be sure of yourselves, but we live in the midst of frailties and uncertainties. You might be well-thought-of by others, but we're mostly kicked around. Much of the time we don't have enough to eat, we wear patched and threadbare clothes, we get doors slammed in our faces, and we pick up odd jobs anywhere we can to eke out a living. When they call us names, we say, 'God bless you.' When they spread rumors about *us*, we put in a good word for *them*. We're treated like garbage, the leftovers that nobody wants. And it's not getting any better." 1 Corinthians 4:9–13 (MSG)

Reflect: How has God been faithful to you? Where has he shown up in the hurt and the hard to reveal his hope and holiness?

God has never
given up on me.
I will not give
up on him.

Intercessors Arising

Day 39

AS I travel the world and get to experience the beauty of the local and global church, I am seeing just how united God's church truly is. I am seeing us get our fight back: intercessors waking up at 3 a.m. and praying without ceasing, sons and daughters preaching the Word of God, and a church that has set their eyes on the real enemy of our souls.

I'm seeing altars full and demons fleeing, prodigals returning, physical healings, broken hearts mending, the bitter forgiving, and the Holy Spirit falling on those desperate for his presence. Somewhere in all our hurt and in all the hard, the anger many have had toward the church has surrendered to the anguish of the saints, rising above all the chaos and confusion of the enemy, who has tried to deceive the people of God, but the truth of God's Word has prevailed.

I am seeing those who have walked away come home after falling for the faulty promises of a sin-filled world. I'm watching grown men and women who once carried unforgiveness toward the other fall into each other's arms in forgiveness and reconciliation. I am witnessing pastors and leaders repenting and congregants joining them.

The cries of the intercessors, the tears of our mothers and fathers in the faith, the fasting of the saints, the contending of the shepherds truly protecting the sheep, we are seeing the fruit of their faithfulness.

Don't stop! Keep pressing in! Keep trusting and believing!

Revival will follow repentance, and we will see the holiness of God fall on our generation.

> "The earth is the LORD's, and everything in it. The world and all its people belong to him. For he laid the earth's foundation on the seas and built it on the ocean depths. Who may climb the mountain of the LORD? Who may stand in his holy place? Only those whose hands and hearts are pure, who do not worship idols and never tell lies. They will receive the LORD's blessing and have a right relationship with God their savior. Such people may seek you and worship in your presence, O God of Jacob." Psalm 24:1–6

Activate: What is God laying on your heart as you pray for your pastors and Christians around the world taking the Great Commission to the far ends of the earth?

Don't stop!
Keep pressing in!
Keep trusting
and believing!

I'm Still Here

Day 40

IT'S been tempting to quit, this I know. To do something easier, less gut wrenching, heart exposing, soul crushing, mind battling. But you're still here too. We've driven through Starbucks and considered the coffee-filled life of a full-time barista, pondered the mystery of a 9-to-5, scrolled social media to see our friends at a carefree Sunday morning brunch, but you're still here. I just think you need to know it's pretty amazing you haven't quit. That thing God has asked you to do, you're still doing it. And most likely at a cost, one that hasn't gone unrecognized by all of heaven, even if nobody else seems to notice. You're still here. So maybe now is a good time to remind the enemy we might be tired, we may have no idea what is next, we might feel overwhelmed or underwhelmed, but we haven't quit and that means something.

Patient endurance. The church needs your patient endurance. Let us sing into the early morning that no weapon formed against us has prospered. May our song remind those weakened by battles and betrayal that God isn't finished with us yet. Wake up, a new day of mercies await you.

I'm still here. You're still here. We're still here.

> "Now may the God of peace make you holy in every way, and may your whole spirit and soul and body be kept blameless until our Lord Jesus Christ comes again. God will make this happen, for he who calls you is faithful." 1 Thessalonians 5:23–24

Still here: How has God sustained you all these years? Below, give him thanks for his faithfulness and great love even in your wavering faith or disbelief. Then use the following pages to reflect on your hurt and hard, and his hope and holy. He is so good.

I'm still here.
You're still here.
We're still here.

My
Hurt

My
Hard

His
Hope

His
Holy